MAIN STREET MILLIONAIRES

***THEY SAY THAT EXPERIENCE IS
THE BEST TEACHER.***

And when it comes to personal investing, the half century's experience by the National Association of Investors Corporation is pretty hard to beat.

This organization, founded by a handful of far-seeing men and women who believed the surest way to insure democracy was to create a financially secure citizenry, has produced thousands of millionaires and is continuing to do so, even as the markets toss and turn and confound today's pundits and politicians.

This is the story of a revolution in personal investment that shook the power corridors of the world's financial communities — the concept that everyday men and women with the patience and commitment to follow sound investment principles could navigate the turbulent waters of high finance and successfully handle their own investments.

Main Street Millionaires is also the inspiring story of Tom O'Hara, who grew up in the midst of the Great Depression to himself become a millionaire several times over, a man guided by faith and integrity and a generous

unyielding passion to share with others the secret of financial success.

But the NAIC way is not a get-rich-quick method. The original investment principles were developed over 60 years ago by a Harvard-trained broker named George Nicholson who used O'Hara and a group of his college chums as experiments for his pioneering group investment theories.

Opposition from the Wall Street power mongers and the big brokerage houses was fierce. Those who controlled the nation's investment procedures had elaborate systems that made it all but impossible for the individual investor or a small club to do their own buying and selling.

But O'Hara and his band of believers broke down those walls, in the process creating a vibrant, growing organization that today has more than 35,000 clubs and a half million members who've used the power of collaboration to take the mystery out of common stock investing.

A half-century's experience has seen the NAIC principles proven many times over, in Bull and Bear markets.

Anyone can be a Main Street Millionaire.

Mike Wendland is a newspaper columnist with the Detroit Free Press, a technology correspondent for 215 NBC-TV Newschannel affiliates and a daily radio commentator. He is a Fellow at the Poynter Institute in St. Petersburg, FL and lives in suburban Detroit.

©2001 National Association of Investors Corporation

From little acorns grow:

MAIN STREET MILLIONAIRES

By Mike Wendland

Contents

Author's Foreword and Acknowledgements

I've got news for you.

You can be rich.

Really.

You don't need special connections or inside information or a lot of money to make money.

It isn't who you are, who you know or how much you have.

Anyone can be rich.

There is no secret.

In fact, the keys to getting rich are so easy to follow that over the past fifty years, literally millions of people, most of them average folks with no specialized educational or vocational backgrounds, have found financial independence, security and wealth by following the common sense investment principles handed down by the National Association of Investors Corporation (NAIC), the organization whose story this book tells in the following pages.

Many of the people who have aligned themselves with NAIC have become millionaires. Over the course of writing this story, I have met a number of them. They are farmers, teachers, factory workers, retirees, truck drivers, computer technicians, housewives, small business owners and secretaries.

Everyday people.

There is a vast community of NAIC members all over the world. I've talked with them online, met them at NAIC conventions and meetings and asked them the questions I needed to understand this association of investment clubs. The thing that has impressed me the most is how generous they are in sharing what they learned.

I'm a pretty skeptical guy. As a journalist with over twenty-five years experience, I've learned the hard way not to believe everything

I've been told. But I started to apply NAIC principles to my own personal financial life and found, to my amazement, that they work. And, perhaps even more amazing for someone who has never liked math or detail work, they are actually fun to apply.

This book tells the story of NAIC over its first half-century. But it is also a personal story about the great men who founded this great organization.

The first is George Nicholson, the late Harvard-educated securities analyst who dreamed of educating the masses about investment, thus strengthening the nation he loved. Here is a man who rubbed shoulders with the great movers and shakers of the financial world on Wall Street, but who always cared first for those who lived on Main Street.

The second is Tom O'Hara, NAIC's Chairman of the Board, a modest man whose strong personal faith and work ethic enabled him to rise from the tough depression-era streets of Detroit to become one of the most generous and caring men I have ever met.

The third is Ken Janke, a man who started his career as a professional golfer in the military. Janke's keen analytical mind was a perfect match for business and economics and has led him to become known far and wide as "Mr. NAIC," always ready to help anyone with advice.

For fifty years now, through times of depression, inflation and recession, through bear markets and bull markets, through wars and political crises, gasoline shortages, and the technology revolution, NAIC has unwaveringly held to its principles of personal investment.

And those principles have never failed. Not once.

They will work for you, too.

In preparing this work, I must thank Tom O'Hara and Ken Janke, who graciously provided me lots of personal time and access to an unpublished memoir by Mr. O'Hara, as well as its forward written by Mr. Janke. Eleanor O'Hara, Tom's wife of more than 50 years, helped me immeasurably with her recollections of the early years. Don Danko, the highly skilled editor of NAIC's *Better Investing* magazine, and Mark Robertson, a senior writer at the magazine, assisted with previously published material and back issues of the publication, particularly some historic material penned by the late

Mr. Nicholson. I also thank Beth Nicholson Hamm, Mr. Nicholson's daughter; and NAIC pioneers Art Baske, Lew Rockwell and Norm Hill for their input and suggestions. At NAIC headquarters, Carole DiFranco, Mary Lawson, Sue Peterman and Bonnie Schmidt provided fast, accurate and great assistance on numerous occasions. Finally, thanks to Bob Larson, of the Larson Communications Group, for putting me in touch with NAIC in the first place.

As I write this, Tom O'Hara is eighty-five years old. He is as sharp and active and interested in the organization he helped found as ever. In fact, he recently made a guest appearance in one of those famous and funny AFLAC "talking duck" television commercials. But even Tom won't be around forever. Each day in America, one thousand people of Tom's generation are passing away. However, as the pages of this book reveal, Tom's legacy will live on, long after he departs this life for the next.

NAIC will be his living monument, a testimony to principled, ethical, disciplined living and investing in a world that very much needs just that sort of direction.

— *Mike Wendland,*
August 2000

Chapter One: Out of the Depression

"...the only thing we have to fear is fear itself"

Tom O'Hara didn't know what to say to the men. He saw them most days on his way home from school, his hands filled with high school textbooks, his coat pulled tight up under his chin as he walked the snowy streets of Southwest Detroit. Sometimes, his school chums were with him and they, too, seemed bothered by the men. The schoolboys would cast their eyes down and whistle, or pretend to be in deep conversation until they had passed by.

Nobody knew what to say. What could they say?

Tom O'Hara didn't think it polite to ignore them. So he did what he always did when at a loss for words. He just smiled. Sometimes, the men would catch his eye and smile back. More often than not, though, they would shift uncomfortably and avoid eye contact.

They were everywhere. Men with grim faces, bundled up in woolen coats and caps. On cold days, icicles sometimes hung from their mustaches as the warmth of their breath caught in the hair and quickly froze. Some men looked angry. Others looked ashamed. They didn't say much. They just stood there along Fort Street, Junction Avenue and on Michigan Avenue, near the streetcar stops, usually up against buildings or in doorways to keep out the chill. Sometimes, they gathered in bunches as a fire blazed in an old metal barrel.

But usually, they stood off alone. Before the winter cold came, they'd often have apples to sell. Or flowers. But with winter, it was usually pencils. Or little homemade paper American flags that could be pinned to a lapel. A few just held an old soup can with the label peeled off, or an empty tobacco can, in case anyone would drop in a coin.

Tom O'Hara wished he had a coin.

But at least his dad was still working, though Robert O'Hara, who tended the turbines for the Detroit City power plant, was paid in script, not real money. They called it "Detroit Dollars." For the city of Detroit, like most everyplace else in America, was basically bankrupt. Still, the Kroger grocery chain accepted Detroit Dollars as cash. So did the big Hudson's department store downtown. Tom O'Hara heard his parents talk in hushed and worried tones around the dinner table downstairs. He knew his dad's salary had been cut drastically. But as he heard his father say so many times, at least he was still working. At least they had food on the table.

Not like so many others. Every day walking home from school, Tom O'Hara would see a half dozen of them at least, begging for money or selling their apples and pencils. The apples for a nickel. The pencils for a penny. These men, young O'Hara often thought, were also dads. They were much more than the "jobless armies" that the Detroit Times called them in their editorials. They were uncles and cousins and brothers and sometimes even grandfathers. They had hungry kids at home. Worried wives.

Tom O'Hara wished he had something to give.

So he smiled at them, warmly, sincerely, blue eyes twinkling, — hoping that the men knew he wished them well. His smile came

6

quick. It was a smile that everybody noticed. Even at seventeen, Tom O'Hara knew that you could say more with a warm smile than with a lot of words. Everyone loved his smile. And so, with nothing else to give these haunting men on the way home from school each day, he gladly gave them his smile.

But deep inside, the plight of these men made him sad. How had things gotten so bad?

It was the second week of March 1933, the fourth year of what the newspapers and the radio were already calling "The Great Depression." Across America, sixteen million people — one third of the nation's work force — were unemployed. Businesses failed. Banks went belly up. O'Hara and his classmates at Detroit Southwestern High School learned all about it in their civics class. There were all sorts of causes, their teacher told them: overproduction of goods; a tariff and war-debt policy from the recently-concluded conflict in Europe that later became known as World War I that curtailed foreign markets for American goods; and easy money policies that led to over expansion of credit and fantastic speculation on the stock market.

The stock market.

That's what everybody really blamed.

It all began not quite five years before. Everything changed. Everything.

In his upstairs bedroom in the rented bungalow where O'Hara lived with his parents, he kept the newspaper and magazine clippings. Tom O'Hara wanted to be a businessman. He knew there were important lessons being played out on the pages of the Detroit News and the Detroit Times and out of this economic disaster. He knew that someday he'd have to understand what had happened to him if he was to be a successful businessman.

Economics fascinated him, though he was hard pressed to explain why. No one else in his blue-collar family had shown any interest or aptitude in business. Especially his dad, who often talked about all those poor people who lost everything they had in the market or in failed banks. In fact, Robert O'Hara distrusted banks so much that for years he refused to buy a house, even though his wife, Olga, delicately broached the subject several times before the big market crash. Tom heard his parents discuss this many times. His Dad was adamant, saying that because of the interest rates, the house would end up costing three times more. So the O'Haras rented instead of buying. When the market collapsed, banks foreclosed on delinquent mortgages and people began losing their homes all around them, Robert O'Hara felt vindicated. The O'Haras still had a roof over their heads. But young Tom, an only child, kept reading everything he could get his hands on about being a businessman. For indeed, there was a lot to learn from the Great Depression.

The newspapers kept referring to the day the stock market crashed as "Black Tuesday." October 29, 1929. But Tom O'Hara knew that October 29 was just the bottom of the fall. It had actually started the week before as prices plummeted. The real day of the crash, O'Hara thought, was "Black Thursday," October 25, 1929. The day the stocks listed on the New York Stock Exchange lost four billion dollars in value. The fall was so dramatic exchange clerks worked until five o'clock in the morning of the next day to clear all the transactions. By the following Monday, when the market re-opened, the realization of what had happened soaked in, and a full-blown panic erupted. The next day, October 29, the market completely collapsed. The newspaper clippings in Tom O'Hara's bedroom recounted the story in grim detail. Tens of thousands of investors were financially ruined. Across the country, businessmen who had lost everything committed suicide by jumping out of their skyscraper offices. By the end of 1929, more than fifteen billion dollars in investments had been wiped out.

Everything happened so fast.

Before the crash, few cities anywhere in the world had seen the economic boom times that Detroit had experienced. Henry Ford had invented the automobile assembly line some fifteen years before and tens of thousands of people had moved to Detroit for the well-paying jobs in the auto factories. Just a few miles from O'Hara's home in Southwest Detroit was Ford's massive River Rouge Factory, the largest industrial complex in history. Here the marvels of mass assembly line production techniques allowed fifty thousand auto workers to produce six thousand cars a day. Other automobile companies developed and flourished all across the city, producing 5,337,000 vehicles in 1929. For more than a decade leading up to the crash, the whole city of Detroit was flush with money. You could see it on the skyline. Two of those auto companies, General Motors and the Fisher Body Company, built huge skyscrapers for their corporate headquarters. Downtown, the opulent new Penobscot building towered forty-seven stories above Griswold and Fort streets in the city's bustling financial district. A mile-long tunnel opened for automobile traffic under the Detroit River to connect the Motor City with the Canadian city of Windsor, Ontario. Streetcars ran on gleaming new tracks and everyone bought a car, luxurious radios, and new clothes. They called the decade the Roaring Twenties.

And then, two months before the end of the decade, it all came to a sudden and devastating end. Those well-paying jobs had brought easy credit but when the market crashed, everyone was caught off guard.

Big businesses and corporations had overextended their reach as much as the working man. As bills came due there simply wasn't enough cash to cover the obligations. Layoffs and salary cuts were almost instantaneous. By 1930, car production was down to 3,363,000. By 1931, seven Detroit auto companies were bankrupt. In August, Ford himself stopped making cars, and sixty thousand laid off workers joined the one hundred thousand already on the street. From there, the crisis mushroomed.

So many people lost jobs that the city didn't know how to respond. They opened up registration centers and counted nearly a quarter million jobless. At Fort and 23rd Street, just a few blocks from Tom O'Hara's home, the once bustling Fisher Body automobile plant was idled and turned into the City Municipal Lodging House. Nearly 2,500 jobless and homeless men were provided heat, light, showers and meals. Almost every store offered a donation barrel for clothing. The men lucky enough to work at Hudson Motor Car Company cut fabric from seat covers to make boy's shirts. Churches and missions set up soup kitchens. On the east side the Capuchin friars fed nearly one thousand people a day. People prayed for snow because the City of Detroit hired thousands of men to shovel snow off roads and sidewalks, paying them two dollars a day in script.

Tensions ran high. The previous year, on March 7, 1932, three thousand men marched towards the sprawling Ford Motor Company headquarters in Dearborn, on Detroit's western boundary, whipped up into an angry mob by organizers of the American Communist Party. Called the Ford Hunger March, they demanded to be rehired and unionized. When Dearborn police attempted to stop them at the border, rioting left four marchers dead and hundreds injured.

So many people were evicted from their homes by banks desperate to collect unpaid mortgages that Clark Park, just a couple of blocks from Tom O'Hara's home, a place where Tom and his buddies played tennis, was turned into a tent city. All around Detroit and across the country, in parklands and empty fields, shanty towns made out of cardboard boxes and wooden crates housed tens of thousands of people. They were derisively called "Hoovervilles," after Herbert Hoover, inaugurated the thirty-first President of the United States just six months before the crash. Many nights Tom O'Hara heard the President's voice on the radio, preaching "rugged individualism" as the cure for the economic mess. It was not a popular message. In 1932, voters booted Hoover. Franklin Delano Roosevelt replaced him on March 4, 1933, promising a "New Deal" of prompt, vigorous action to end the Great Depression.

Tom O'Hara anxiously read about all of this, and listened to the new President discuss his "hundred day" plan on the radio.

In his inaugural address, Roosevelt spoke boldly and with optimistic confidence to a shell-shocked nation.

"This great Nation will endure as it has endured, will revive and will prosper," promised the new president. *"So, first of all, let me assert my firm belief that the only thing we have to fear is fear itself — nameless, unreasoning, unjustified terror which paralyzes needed efforts to convert retreat into advance."*

This speech greatly affected Tom O'Hara's young mind, especially when Roosevelt, in his high-pitched but warm and authoritative voice, talked about the proper view of money.

"Happiness lies not in the mere possession of money; it lies in the joy of achievement, in the thrill of creative effort. The joy and moral stimulation of work no longer must be forgotten in the mad chase of

evanescent profits. These dark days will be worth all they cost us if they teach us that our true destiny is not to be ministered unto but to minister to ourselves and to our fellow men."

Tom O'Hara was inspired. Indeed just as he had already concluded, the lessons emerging from this Great Depression, if properly applied, would benefit the common good. The President of the United States had just said the very thing that Tom O'Hara concluded as a youth of seventeen. Better times lay ahead. They really did. Tom O'Hara knew it. He was optimistic for those jobless men with the apples and pencils that he passed everyday. And he was optimistic about his own future. He would become a businessman, he was sure of it. A businessman who, like the new President urged, used his success, not for his own gain, but for the good of his fellow man.

Tom O'Hara was a popular young man. He was his high school class valedictorian and very active in school. Everyone knew him for his smile. He was popular with younger and older classmates alike and enjoyed a wide circle of friends. He kept confidences and never said a negative thing about anyone. To this day, that's one of the things everyone who has ever spent time with Tom O'Hara says, he doesn't gossip.

As a teenager, his life revolved around tennis. Every summer, he and his friends woke up at four in the morning and trudged a mile from their neighborhood to the tennis courts at a city park along the Detroit River. They played from sunup to suppertime. He frequented the YMCA and the Military Avenue Presbyterian Church, where he attended Sunday School and actively participated in the youth group.

One of his best friends from church was a boy named George Palmer. Although they were the same age and lived close to each other, Palmer attended Western High School and had an entirely different set of friends than Tom O'Hara, who went to Southwestern High. But besides their friendship at church, the two shared a common interest.

Both were fascinated by business in general and investing in particular. They often talked about the profound effects of the Great Depression and wondered how they'd ever get enough money to someday get married and buy an automobile. They knew that they needed to amass enough money to eliminate dependence on a fickle economy. The only way they figured that could happen was if they learned how to invest wisely and actually own shares of healthy, growing businesses. That meant the stock market.

But they didn't share this with their friends and families. Such talk would bring ridicule. Too many people had been ruined in the crash of 1929. Banks remained closed and men on street corners still sold apples and pencils. Talk about buying stock would sound foolish. O'Hara and Palmer kept their plans to themselves.

In fact, throughout 1933 and 1934, as their high school years came to an end. And as the effects of the Great Depression lingered on, the two secretly kept imaginary portfolios on stocks. They eagerly rushed home from classes to grab the *Detroit Times* and look up the latest reports. Tom knew that college awaited. And eventually, marriage. Yet many nights he heard his parents talk about the uncertainties of the economy. On holidays and at family gatherings, other relatives, too, shared their frustrations about making do with less. During the height of the Great Depression, wages were continuously lowered. It seemed like every other month wages were being reduced by five dollars a week.

Tom's Dad was lucky to make $40 a week. From that $160 or so a month, he paid $50 for rent and $30 for a family automobile. They were fortunate. Food always graced their table. Good food, too, nutritional meals supplemented by vegetables canned by his Mom, Olga. But restaurants were forbidden. Worn out clothes were mended. When Tom and his friends planned to go somewhere, it took some doing to scrounge together ten cents for a gallon of gasoline.

The summer before his senior year in high school, Tom and his pals had participated in a YMCA trip to the wilderness island of Isle Royale, located in the middle of Lake Michigan between the Upper Peninsula of Michigan and the western shore of Wisconsin. The trip cost twenty dollars, a small fortune to a seventeen year-old boy from a city hard hit by the Great Depression. Tom scrimped and saved, ran errands, cut lawns, and cleaned out garages to earn his share. It took him nearly six months. It was worth it. The trip was the adventure of a lifetime. Few paved roads existed outside of big cities and the truck the teens drove to the Upper Peninsula thumped with a flat tire seemingly every half-dozen miles.

Still they made it. And even though a severe storm stranded the young men on the island for several extra days, it was one of those character-building times that shaped Tom O'Hara's life. He learned he could meet financial goals. Working hard, saving and focusing on the ultimate reward of the trip convinced Tom O'Hara that he could determine his financial future. And being with a fun-loving group of friends who similarly worked, saved and learned how to determine and hit a financial target taught them all that the process is fun.

Tom O'Hara played the stock market. He had no money, of course. But each night he poured over the stock market reports in the newspaper and pretended to buy. He devoured everything he could find about investing. And though all the adults in his life made it clear that the stock market caused the terrible condition of the nation, Tom O'Hara knew better. On paper, his imaginary portfolio made money. George Palmer's pretend holdings also prospered. Both young men were excited about what they were learning. They believed that owning stock was truly the way to build wealth, even in the middle of an economic depression the likes of which the world had never seen before. The two had no idea how to select stocks except by watching the firms whose value kept increasing. Those that prospered when all the others staggered offered products that served a real need. They were well merchandised and advertised. Companies that sold clothing. Automobiles. Food and groceries. Tom's rule of thumb was that if it was in the O'Hara cupboard or closet or driveway, the company that made that product was probably worth owning.

"If only we actually had enough money to really buy some stock," Palmer said one day.

"How much do you reckon we'd need?" asked O'Hara.

"At least ten or twenty dollars every month. Even if you and I put everything together that we earned from our after school jobs for six months, there's no way we'd be able to raise that much. Not in these times."

O'Hara's wheels were turning. "What if we got ten or twenty of our buddies to join us? We could pool all our spare change, just like we do when I get my dad's car and we need to buy gas. Instead, we'll buy stock."

The two agreed to quietly approach a couple of friends at their different high schools to sound them out. They did not get much encouragement.

"Everyone wants to make money," O'Hara told Palmer one afternoon after school. "But everybody says their parents would kill 'em if they heard they were wasting money by tossing it in the stock market."

Palmer got the same response. "Nobody sees any future in stocks."

O'Hara nodded. "Nobody except you and me."

"Yeah and they think we're nuts to even suggest such a thing after what happened in '29. Guess we're behind the times, Tom. Too late with too little."

"Too bad. Maybe someday."

Tom O'Hara and George Palmer were kids. All this talk of owning stock and investing was a hobby. Something to dream about. As the end of their senior year drew near, O'Hara and Palmer saw each other less and less. Graduation approached. Both young men knew they had to go to college. Palmer's family seemed to be solid enough financially, despite the tough times, to assume the extra costs the following September.

It was a different story for Tom O'Hara. A few months before his eighteenth birthday, he was facing a dilemma that threatened to cut short all of his dreams. If only the couple of hundred dollars Tom's imaginary portfolio had "made" were real, it would have been so easy. But as his high school years came to an end, he had something else very much on his mind.

There was no money to go to college.

Tom wanted to attend Wayne State University in downtown Detroit and major in Business Administration. But his family didn't have the fifty dollars needed for tuition. It had taken Tom months of work to earn twenty dollars for the Isle Royale trip the summer before. Mentally, he beat himself up many nights over that. Maybe he shouldn't have spent it on such a fleeting fancy. Maybe he should have saved it. But he didn't. He couldn't turn back the clock anymore than he could cash in his imaginary stock investments. The money his family thought all along would be there to send Tom to college, wasn't. The Depression showed no signs of easing up.

In the midst of it all, O'Hara had a friend whose family seemed untouched by the depression. Bud Peterson was his name and his father owned the Precision Spring Company. The plant sprawled across an entire city block on Telegraph Road just across the city's northern boundary of Eight Mile Road. Peterson lived in a mansion in an exclusive part of Detroit called Palmer Woods and O'Hara was sure that Peterson's father was a millionaire. The family didn't live ostentatiously, but O'Hara saw what wealth could bring. They were secure. Unworried by the economic troubles that gripped the Motor City. The Petersons were generous and often took Tom and a number of other friends out to a fine restaurant. He was impressed that they could spend as much on a meal as the O'Hara's weekly budget.

During those visits, Peterson's father, Alfred Peterson Sr., often shared his philosophy. Money, he said, made money. Money was not to be squandered. It was to be nurtured. Invested.

After dinner, returning to the Peterson's home and seated around the finished basement floor, young Tom O'Hara and other friends received impromptu lectures on politics and economics by their friend's father. The one thing Mr. Peterson wanted O'Hara and his friends to know was that they should never, never invest in the stock market. Peterson, it seemed, had a bad experience. One of the reasons he had time to lecture high school kids was because he had sold his company not long before. The firm that bought it paid him some cash and a lot of stock. As part of the deal, that stock could not be sold for five or six years. When he received the stock it was worth some thirty five dollars a share. Thanks to the Depression, it had sunk to less than a dollar a share.

Peterson was very leery of stocks.

O'Hara listened and thought about the long term. Someday, he thought to himself, that stock would go back up in value. Even then, the depression was clearly bottoming out. There was no way to go but up. O'Hara paid close attention to Mr. Peterson yet decided that, while he needed to be careful with stocks, investing in companies that produced something people wanted, just made good sense.

What O'Hara needed most was fifty dollars. Tom O'Hara was not going to give up his dream of attending college. Somehow, he would raise the tuition money himself. Although a quarter-million Detroiters were out of work, he set out to find a job. Just as he picked his imaginary stocks based on companies that sold in-demand products, he similarly targeted his prospective employer. It was a factory called Universal Cooler. They made what appeared to be a depression-proof product, electric refrigerators. The company manufactured private brand units for dozens of companies. However their biggest client was one of Tom's growth stock choices in his pretend investment holdings — Sears Roebuck & Co.

Universal Cooler hired Tom as mail boy. He earned ten dollars a week, a nearly miraculous sum since it was part time work and so many men were unemployed. He squirreled away every cent he made. Maybe, just maybe, after helping out his parents with the family budget, spending a buck or two a week on streetcars and buses and a movie or Detroit Tigers baseball game every now and then — maybe he'd be able to save enough to pay his college tuition. But it would take him a whole year, he grimly calculated. At least.

He made up his mind to do it and the weeks and months slowly passed. The landlord sold the Southwest Detroit house the family had rented for years. They moved into a flat for about a year. Some of his friends drifted away. Some went to college. Nearly every cent Tom made was taken up in just living. Welcome to the real world. Still he did it. He buckled down and, for a year, he put in his time at Universal Cooler. He put away his dimes, nickels, quarters and dollars until, in mid 1934, he had saved the fifty dollars.

He entered Wayne State University that fall and quickly settled into college life, attending classes, riding buses and streetcars to the downtown campus of Wayne State. Although Tom's father had always been dead set against buying a house on credit and paying interest on a mortgage, his wife felt differently. When her father died, he left her a small inheritance, just enough, she figured, to make a down payment on a house. So, after Mrs. O'Hara convinced her husband to change his mind, the O'Hara family became homeowners on Mendotta Street, near Seven Mile Road in northwest Detroit.

In Tom's freshman year, at a sorority dance, he fell head-over-heels for a girl named Eleanor Urquhart. The only problem was, she was someone else's date. In fact, Tom had set her up with his friend, Bud Peterson. Tom couldn't take his eyes off her all night.

He asked her out the next week, and all through college they spent as much time together as they could. But it wasn't much. There wasn't a lot of time for either of them. The college years rushed by.

Tom O'Hara needed to earn money and, right after his graduation, landed a job in the purchasing department first at the General Electric Supply Company and then at Kelvinator Supply Company, on Fort Street, back in southwest Detroit. O'Hara's family was strapped for cash. Surviving the Great Depression had taken every cent they could muster and now, with the extra cost of a mortgage, the family needed Tom's help. By this time, Tom took home about twenty dollars a week and gave as much as he could to his parents.

Eleanor's situation was even worse. Her father had recently died and her younger brother and sister still lived at home. She, too, felt obligated to work and help her mother. She was a secretary for the personnel manager of a Detroit-based oil company.

One day, at Eleanor's house, Tom waited in the living room. Eleanor was in her room, getting ready for their date. The younger children were laughing and giggling and running about. Eleanor's mother came into the living room and sat down. She looked right at Tom and sighed. She knew the couple was getting serious. She liked Tom. She liked him a lot. But she also knew this was not the time for them to get serious. Gently, but firmly, Eleanor's mother gave Tom a lesson in the economic realities of post-Depression America.

"Tom," she said, "these are tough times. And it's awful hard to get along in this world. Do you know how much it takes for a family to get by?"

Tom didn't. But Eleanor's mother, Mrs. Urquhart did. "It takes an income of about three thousand dollars a year. You're making twenty dollars a week. That adds up to a little over one thousand dollars. And you need to use some of that to help your parents."

Young Tom O'Hara didn't say much. He nodded politely. Inside, his heart ached. When he and Eleanor went out later that night, they had a tough decision to make. Reluctantly, they realized they had to put their relationship on the back burner while they helped their families. Though both wanted to spend more time together, family circumstances and the work demands on their time made that impossible.

It was not a happy time for either of them. But they had to make the sacrifice to stop seeing each other. It required discipline. They had to put their dreams on hold.

"It will all work out some day," Tom said, taking Eleanor's hand and smiling. "It really will."

"Some day," said Eleanor, also smiling, but through tear-filled eyes and a quivering lower lip. "Some day."

Bud Peterson had a proposition. O'Hara was a sophomore at Wayne State and the two sat side-by side in a history class. The professor was down front in the auditorium lecturing. O'Hara was half dozing.

"Psst, Tom," Peterson whispered. O'Hara nodded himself alert, at first wondering if the professor had seen him with his head down.

"What?" O'Hara was glad he was undetected but mildly irritated that he had been aroused.

"I don't know what you're getting out of all this college stuff, but I've had it. I'm going to start my own business."

O'Hara looked at his friend blankly.

"My dad has given me a stake," Peterson explained. He reached down into his bookbag and brought out a little booklet. Embossed on the cover were two words: Detroit Bank. It had Peterson's name as the account holder. He tossed it on O'Hara's desk.

"Go ahead. Open it."

Puzzled, O'Hara opened the bank book. It showed a single deposit. For one million dollars.

O'Hara gulped. His pal Bud Peterson was a millionaire.

"I'm going to use that to start my own business and I want you to come and work for me."

The professor ended his lecture. The conversation continued. The two stayed in the auditorium. Peterson shared his plan. He would drop out of college. His Dad had given him lots of advice besides the million dollars, he explained, and he was going to start a company that would build valves and springs for the automobile companies.

"I'll run it and I want you to be my right-hand man," said Peterson.

O'Hara thought about it. But not for long. Bud Peterson was one of his best friends. But somehow, working for his friend had never figured into Tom's plans. Besides, Peterson's father was a controlling man. O'Hara knew that the father would dominate the son. O'Hara had spent a lot of time with the Petersons. He knew they liked him a lot. He knew that Mr. Peterson had probably already given his son permission to ask Tom to join him. Yet no matter how inviting it all appeared, Tom knew that his name was O'Hara and their name was Peterson and whatever business Bud started would always be a family business. A Peterson family business.

O'Hara turned his friend down.

Bud tried several times to persuade Tom to change his mind. Then, with a handshake, Peterson said he understood. He picked another friend from school to take Tom's place. Soon, both had quit their classes and moved to Three Rivers, Michigan. Over the next couple of years, O'Hara received reports about Peterson. The plant was quickly up and running and enjoying brisk business. Eventually, Bud Peterson would make many millions on his own and control more than a dozen manufacturing facilities scattered across the globe.

O'Hara's decision to refuse the job never affected their relationship. They remained lifelong friends.

One day in December 1939, Tom O'Hara was delighted to find his old pal George Palmer at the door. They hadn't seen each other for some time and after catching up, Palmer got to the point.

"Remember that crazy idea you had back in high school about starting a stock market club?" Palmer asked.

O'Hara had to think a bit. Before the reality had sunk in about the lack of college tuition, back when he and Palmer were pretending to be big shot tycoons by following the newspaper financial sections, he had indeed wondered if there was a group of chums from school that could get together and start some sort of club. Maybe they could even chip in a half-buck each and if enough of them could pool part of their allowances or income from part time jobs, maybe they could actually buy some stock, make some investments.

"Yeah, I remember," said O'Hara. "We realized that none of the kids we knew, including us, had two nickels to rub together. It was just a silly idea."

"Well," said Palmer, leaning closer, "maybe it's not so silly after all."

Palmer said he had recently met someone who shared an interest in the stock market. "And you're not going to believe it, Tom. This fellow, Fred Russell is his name, Fred says he wants to start a club, an investment club, where everybody gets together and kicks in a couple of bucks and picks a stock to buy. He is calling a group together next week. He asked me to bring anyone that might be interested and I thought of you."

Tom O'Hara had two reactions.

He was excited, remembering his old dreams of financial security through investing. His heart beat faster. Maybe the idea wasn't so bad after all. Others apparently thought it made sense. He pictured the penciled columns of imaginary investments he had made in his bedroom back in high school, following the financial section of the newspaper. Suppose it really worked? He imagined the neatly entered columns of ever-increasing numbers. Then he pictured Eleanor. If this investment idea was successful, he could marry her. His heart soared.

Then it plummeted. He faced his financial reality. He had been working at his second job since graduation from college the year before. And this job, as a junior assistant with the Ernst & Ernst accounting firm in downtown Detroit, paid only eighteen dollars a week — two dollars less than he had earned at Kelvinator. He had taken the job for the experience and the possibility of advancement. However, he was already hoping to move on. A college professor suggested a job with the city and Tom applied to the accounting department at the Detroit Board of Education. But even if he got that job and a slight raise, his family situation had not changed.

"What's the matter?" asked Palmer, seeing the sudden downturn in Tom's face.

"How much is this going to cost?"

"Well, we're hoping we can get everyone to kick in ten bucks a month. That way we can build a pretty good investment." Palmer tossed out the figure like it was nothing. He came from a fairly well-off family and to him it was a modest sum.

For Tom O'Hara, it might as well have been a hundred dollars.

O'Hara smiled and sighed. "George, I still don't have two nickels to rub together. I can't possibly come up with ten dollars a month."

Palmer wasn't having any of that from his pal. "Aw, Tom, don't worry. We'll figure out something. Just come to the meeting. Let's see what happens."

O'Hara had his doubts. But he was also curious. He was excited to see his old idea of an investment club coming true. He wouldn't miss the opportunity to attend the meeting for the world. He agreed and, several days later, went with his old friend to the evening meeting.

Fred Russell hosted the meeting in his home. Like most young men out of college and in their early twenties, Russell still lived with his parents.

Like O'Hara, Russell had been a business major in college. He graduated from Wheaton College, near Chicago, and, although the two had never met, Tom instantly liked the smiling, confident, well-dressed young man who greeted him at the door. George made the introductions.

"I've heard about you, Tom O'Hara," beamed Fred Russell. "You're a man with a good head on your shoulders. George tells me you had an idea for a group like this when the two of you were just kids. You're going to like what I have to say tonight."

Over the course of a half hour, another half dozen young men in their early twenties trooped up the Russell front porch and rang the bell. Several had just come from their jobs and hungrily looked around for the crackers and snacks prepared by Russell's mother, before she retired to another room, her husband, and the rest of the family, to "let you young men have your meeting."

Except for Palmer, Tom O'Hara didn't know any of them. Russell, it soon became apparent, knew most of the boys who filled up the house. From their conversation, O'Hara learned that most knew each other from high school. They had attended Western High, like Palmer, and had grown up together. They all liked sports. O'Hara overheard several of them reminiscing about touch football games they had played.

It was time to get the meeting started.

"You know the rules," smiled Fred. "No smoking, no cussin', no drinking." There were some snickers and good-natured ribbing. One of the men patted his vest where, like many others, he had a flask, even in the midst of Prohibition.

A young man standing next to Tom O'Hara chuckled. "Fred's a teetotaler," whispered the man. He motioned with his head to the other room, where the family was. "Fred's dad in there is a Baptist minister."

O'Hara didn't know what to say. He smiled and stuck out his hand and introduced himself to the stranger, who in turn introduced himself. "I'm Norm Hill," he said. "I work for Mr. George A. Lyon. Lyon Steel. I'm the Quality Control Manager." Hill said it matter-of-factly. "Stainless steel. It's going to be big."

Others introduced themselves. Howard Wilson, worked for the sprawling U.S. Rubber plant that supplied Detroit automobile companies with tires. A big guy named Al Castorri was an accountant. Leo Jacobson said he worked for the City of Detroit Parking Authority. Don Thomas. The names came too fast. O'Hara did his best to keep them all straight.

Russell cleared his throat as the group took their seats on the sofa, in easy chairs, on a piano bench.

"As most of you know," he began, "I have the pleasure of working as a secretary in a downtown brokerage office. The lucky thing for all of us is the man I work for is George A. Nicholson, Jr." Russell paused for effect.

O'Hara had never heard of George A. Nicholson, Jr. Judging by the blank stares from the others, no one else in the group had heard of him either.

Russell quickly sketched out the background of his boss. Nicholson, he explained, was a graduate of Harvard Business School, and while in Boston had learned that there were a good number of organizations called investment clubs in that city. An investment club, Russell patiently explained, was simply a group of individuals who joined together for the purpose of buying stocks. "Just like we're thinking about doing."

Tom O'Hara was excited to hear that his idea really was workable. When he had thought of it back in high school, he hadn't realized that other groups were actually doing what he visualized. He sat forward, eager to hear more from Russell.

"Mr. Nicholson is a very exceptional gentleman," Fred Russell explained, respect evident in the tone of his voice. "He is not only a very astute security analyst, but he is also deeply concerned about the public's lack of knowledge about securities and how to select stocks for investment. He has a great desire, as he frequently has told me, to find a program for mass-education in security ownership. He has the hope that investment clubs can be used in that way. On top of that I want you all to know he is a kindly man and never hesitates to spend time with people who show an interest in being taught a few lessons in investing. If we are to indeed form such a club, I'm sure you will all get the opportunity to meet him."

The young men were paying close attention. Several nodded. Russell continued.

Fred had received excellent guidance from George Nicholson for setting up the potential investment club. He explained that the young men did not have much money and, because several of them had recently married and were just starting out in their careers, it was important they not lose what they had. They were all hoping the new venture would finance honeymoons, make down payments on houses or put kids through school.

"If we are to do this," Russell explained, "we must be very serious. Now I know you boys like to have a good time. In fact, I know there are some of you who have no trouble spending ten dollars a month drinking beer."

There were lots of laughs. Norm Hill in particular laughed long and hard. "Shucks, Fred, that's on a slow month," he guffawed. His buddies laughed even louder. Tom O'Hara smiled. If he had ten dollars he could sure think of better uses for it than guzzling beer, he thought. But he didn't say anything. He was anxious for Russell to keep talking.

"The fact that some of you boys can spend ten dollars a month on beer tells me that you can afford to invest ten dollars a month for your financial security," he said good-naturedly. He again had their attention.

Then he gave them three principles of financial investing that he said came directly from George Nicholson.

"Mr. Nicholson says that if we are to seriously do this, we must seriously commit to these principles. No matter what." He looked around at each of the young men sprawled out in his living room. They were hanging on every word. Tom O'Hara took notes. So did a couple of others.

"The first principle," Russell solemnly explained, "is that we must invest regularly without trying to guess which way the market is going. Mr. Nicholson says that people generally are afraid to buy during down markets, like we've been seeing for many years now. Conversely, people are very happy to buy whenever everything seems easy, as it did in the late Twenties. The result of this is that many people bought their stocks when they were over-priced and did not buy when they were bargains. But Mr. Nicholson says if we buy regularly in all kinds of markets, we'll end up with low average prices and at market peaks we'll tend to have great profits."

There were nods all around the room.

"The second principle Mr. Nicholson says our club must follow is to put compound income to work and make money on money."

There were some puzzled looks. Russell saw them and quickly explained. "That means the club has to reinvest all of our earnings at each monthly meeting. This will keep us fully invested every month and it's another way of keeping us from trying to guess whether or not it is a good time to invest. Since the club will meet every month and have new money on hand each month from your ten dollar contributions, it always will have money to invest in down markets."

There was a third principle, Russell said, and it was perhaps the most important.

"The third principle we must follow is to learn how to select stocks that have the chance to be worth twice as much five years in the future, or the next time the market reaches a new peak. And it will rise again. And fall again. Mr. Nicholson has studied the market very carefully. All we have to be is disciplined and educated about how to select companies in which "to invest."

The third principle sounded like a real stumbling block to the group. How could a bunch of neophytes who had absolutely no real experience in investing possibly learn how to identify stocks that would be capable of that kind of performance?

Russell told them that George Nicholson had anticipated that question. He had developed a system.

"When he was a student learning how to analyze stocks at Harvard, Mr. Nicholson created something he called a Stock Check List. In his securities work, and in his efforts to pick stocks that would produce superior investment results, he reached two very sound conclusions: One was that if a company was going to be worth a lot more in the future, it had to grow its business. That meant increasing its sales and also its earnings per share. Further, Mr. Nicholson reasoned that if a company was going to grow and make money doing it, it had to have a manager or executive with the knowledge, skill and drive to both move the business forward and make money doing it."

Again Russell paused, letting the words sink in. The sound of scribbling pencils filled the room. Eventually, every head looked up at him again. He continued.

"In other words, Mr. Nicholson says profitable growth comes from management. To pick stocks that are likely to grow, we have to identify management capable of producing that growth. And Mr. Nicholson has devised a little tool to test management's ability to grow the business."

It was a piece of paper with a form. Russell showed it to the group. "Mr. Nicholson calls this his management tester," said Russell. "If the company's records come up looking good on this form, this is a sign that management passed his test and is capable of producing the growth we want."

Russell passed the paper around. Then he showed how anyone could analyze company management by looking up stock performance data in the newspaper and at the library and entering the figures.

"We have to do the research," Russell said. "But if we're disciplined and make our investments based on objective facts instead of emotion, if we stick to the principles, we will succeed. It is not unreasonable for us to expect five to seven percent return on our investments."

The group radiated enthusiasm. They had a plan. Many wanted to start right then. Some dug into their wallets. Tom O'Hara wished he had ten dollars. If he was lucky, he had three.

"Wait a minute, boys, not so fast." Russell was grinning. "This isn't something we rush into. Like a marriage, if we form this club, it's for a lifetime. And we need to be very clear about why we are doing this. For me, there are two reasons. One, I want to start my own business someday, and that will require three thousand dollars. That's as much as some of you highly paid boys make in a year. Mr. Nicholson is a wonderful boss, but it will take me decades to save that much working as a secretary. Another reason is I want to have a second income from investments, and I figure the club will eventually provide it. In fact, my personal goal is to have an annual income from dividends of one thousand dollars."

Men gasped all around the room. Could it be possible? Could their ten dollar a month beer money contributions actually result in that much money?

Russell exuded confidence. His face beamed. Clearly, he had every confidence in the world that the club would succeed. The excitement was contagious and one by one Russell asked each man if he wanted to be part of the club, following the principles and stock-picking procedures suggested by George Nicholson, contributing ten dollars a month.

When it came time for Tom O'Hara to vote, his heart ached. He wanted in desperately. But he had no money. Red-faced he explained his situation.

No one cared. "We want you in, Tom," said George Palmer.

"But I can't come up with ten dollars a month right now," said Tom.

"Right now, you say," said his new friend Norm Hill. "But now's not forever."

O'Hara was touched by the sincere acceptance the group offered but it didn't change the fact that he had no money to invest.

Fred Russell cleared his throat.

"Gentlemen, I believe I have the solution," he said. "I propose that Tom be a full member of the group and allowed to attend all of our meetings." There were nods and grunts of agreement all around. Norm Hill patted Tom on the back.

"Tom will be exempted from the ten dollar contribution requirement for three months. At that time, if he is still unable to contribute, his membership will be re-evaluated. Any objections?"

There were none.

Tom was in. He was ecstatic. Secretly, he determined that, somehow, over the next three months, he'd save ten dollars so that he could join the others as a full contributing member.

Christmas came and went and the calendar turned to New Year, 1940. The group met again in January and worked on the letter of agreement they would sign to form the club. On February 1, 1940, what was to eventually become the Mutual Investment Club of Detroit formally came into existence. At that time it was simply The Club.

As the men signed their names and anted up their first ten dollars there was a lot of kidding and laughter.

They had no idea what they had just done.

They had no idea what a positive influence their actions would have on hundreds of thousands of people.

They had no idea how their actions that night in Fred Russell's home would set in motion a movement that, in a very real sense, would determine the economic direction of millions of people across the nation.

On a personal level, this group of high-spirited young men had no idea what it would mean to themselves. They would all become millionaires. Most of them several times over.

Chapter Two: **In Our Mutual Interest**

WWII

Detroit Free Press

FEATURES SECTION

October 17, 1949

**"MUTUAL INVESTMENT
CLUB WORTH
$20,690"**

A s it turned out, Tom O'Hara never did have to scrimp and save to come up with the ten dollar-a-month dues for the Mutual Investment Club. In the spring of 1940, just before his three-month trial membership would have expired, he was hired as an accountant for the Detroit Board of Education at the then-amazing salary of three thousand dollars a year.

The members of the Mutual Investment Club kept meeting every month at Fred Russell's house. If any of the young men who filled the Russell living room in those meetings had an inkling that what they were doing would one day turn them into millionaires, it sure wasn't evident. It soon became apparent that none of them had the slightest idea of what they were doing. In fact, some saw the meeting as an excuse to have a boy's night out, and they couldn't wait for the meetings to end so they could retire to a nearby tavern.

Fred Russell ran the meetings, using topics recommended by George Nicholson as discussion material. Nicholson, Russell explained, understood the young men didn't have much money and couldn't afford to lose the ten dollars a month they were contributing. Instead, members hoped to prosper. There was lots of good natured speculation about what they'd all do with their investments, and they all hoped that, if they were lucky, their investments would one day finance honeymoons, make down payments on houses or put kids through schools.

"It isn't a matter of luck," Russell told them, quoting his mentor, George Nicholson. "It's a matter of discipline." Over and over in those early meetings, Russell, as directed by Nicholson, kept repeating the three principles:

- Invest regularly, without trying to guess which way the market is going.
- Make money on money by not taking out dividends or interest and letting it compound.
- Invest only in companies that seem to offer the potential to double in value every five years.

Nicholson did not attend any of the early meetings of the Mutual Investment Club. It was by design, of course. Although none of the men knew it at the time, and some wondered why this "Mr. Nicholson" spoken of so reverentially by Fred Russell, was so generous in sharing his knowledge. The club was an experiment. A living laboratory to prove out a grand vision. If what these young and happy-go-lucky would-be investors were undertaking really worked out, Nicholson would have a model for what he hoped would become a movement. Since his Harvard days, he had been dreaming of an association of many such clubs, made up of everyday people who would own a stake in the nation's leading corporations. That, figured Nicholson, would make for a stronger America. But before that could happen, individual investors needed to be educated about how the economy works and what assures a successful investment.

From a distance and through Fred Russell, who worked as a secretary at his Detroit brokerage office, Nicholson patiently designed and then directed the slow and steady education of the Mutual Investment Club members. The men needed a sense of ownership. They needed to develop their own investment skills. And Nicholson knew that for that to happen, they'd have to do it on their own.

At the February 1940 meeting, the club made its first stock purchase, Federal Department Stores, a Detroit retail chain. It did very well for years until suburban shopping malls changed the retail market in the sixties and the chain eventually went out of business. But by then the Mutual Investment Club had sold their shares, realizing a handy profit.

In March 1940 the club bought its second stock, investing in Federal Mogul Corporation, an investment it would hold until 1988.

After each monthly meeting, Nicholson relentlessly questioned Russell about what the group said and did, feeding him investment principles to pass on to the group at the next meeting, answering their questions, addressing their concerns and showing them how to identify good management and to spot investment trends.

Part of that educational process involved a proper understanding of the way world events and politics affects capitalism and private industry.

And in those early years of the Mutual Investment Club, the world was offering up some powerful lessons.

Europe was at war.

Although the Austrian-born founder of the German Nazi Party and Chancellor of the Third Reich, Adolph Hitler, had attracted widespread news coverage since he took control in 1934, most people didn't take him seriously until it was too late.

Nicholson was one of the first and few who saw in Hitler a huge threat to the American way of life. American newspapers dismissed Hitler as "the little dictator," and ran editorial cartoons that made him look like Charlie Chaplin, the old star of silent movies. Nicholson knew better and made certain that at each meeting, through Russell, the members of the Mutual Investment Club understood that the growing world turmoil would soon envelop the United States, even though many newspapers were urging a hands-off approach.

In 1939, Hitler and his storm troopers had invaded Poland. Hitler had formed strong and aggressive alliances with Mussolini in Italy and Franco in Spain. Suddenly, Hitler's ruthless and fascist war machine ran roughshod over the entire continent. As Nicholson had predicted, America would soon be drawn into the conflict.

The members of the Mutual Investment Club needed little persuasion. After weeks of intense and heated debate, Congress enacted the first military draft during peacetime. The Selective Training and Service Act went into effect in October 1940 and one by one, with sixteen million other American men between the ages of twenty-one and thirty-five, each member made their way to the Wayne County, Michigan Draft Board to register for military service. Two weeks later, the club members listened to the radio as Secretary of War Henry L. Stimson plucked the first number for the draft from a bowl filled with capsules numbered one to 8,994. The number was 158; 6,175 men across the nation held that honor.

As the European conflict raged, more and more men were called up each month. The first members of the Mutual Investment Club received notice just before Christmas. And as the calendar turned to 1941, at nearly every meeting, one or two others announced that their numbers had been called.

Then came Pearl Harbor. On Sunday, December 7, 1941, without warning, Japanese planes attacked the huge U.S. naval base on the Hawaiian island of Oahu, destroying or severely damaging nineteen naval vessels and some two hundred aircraft. The United States entered World War II the following day.

All of the founding members of the Mutual Investment Club were called into military service. Except one — Fred Russell.

Although Russell was also drafted, he was later rejected for medical reasons. At his military physical, doctors detected a heart murmur. This classified him as 4F, "physically unfit for service."

It was providential.

The drafted club members were scattered all over the globe. Tom O'Hara traveled to Iceland, and later to London. Others went to islands in the Pacific, to South America or were landed aboard ships at sea in the North Atlantic or Pacific theaters.

Only Russell remained back home and, because of that, the club continued. From all over the world, the members in the military continued to mail Russell their monthly checks. In turn, Russell mailed each of them monthly reports of the club's activities and investment holdings. He researched stocks and sent information about promising companies. Despite the chaos of the war, members exchanged ideas and voted by mail. And, unlike other letters received by the sailors and soldiers of the Mutual Investment Club at their various wartime locations, Russell's reports arrived in a relatively timely fashion.

They also piqued the interest of the senior military officers who acted as censors, reading the members' correspondence with Russell. Across the globe, the members all were enthusiastically quizzed by their superior officers about the investment club. Many bluntly asked to join the group. Requests poured into Russell's home back in Detroit. Russell concluded that the paperwork challenge, together with the vagrancies of military mail and the constant location transfers of military personnel, would make it an overwhelming task. Thus the soldiers and sailors from Detroit often found themselves in the difficult position of having to turn down a request from a superior officer. But the fact that newcomers exposed to the investment principles taught by Nicholson were so interested in the concept convinced and excited the club members. Maybe this really was an idea that was bigger than a boy's night out.

Tom O'Hara, stationed on a remote military installation off the Northern coast of Iceland, was particularly impressed. The club's investments seemed to be going well.

Not so with a personal investment he had made. His very first.

Just before he was sent overseas, he sunk $200 into his first independent stock investment, on a whim, he later realized.

He bought stock in Hupp Motor Company because he thought the Huppmobile motorcar was the prettiest car on the road. But while he was in Iceland the company fell on hard times. It stopped making cars. His mother wrote him to express her worry over his failing investment. Finally, when the stock took a sudden but short rise on reports that the company was going to be resurrected as a parts manufacturer, he wrote his Mom back home and told her to sell. It netted $280, a profit of $80.

He was lucky, thought O'Hara in Iceland, very lucky. Even though he made out well, he knew that he bought the stock based purely on emotion. He had a lot to learn. There was safety in numbers. That's why the investment club was such a good idea. With everyone's money at stake, investment decisions could be made more objectively.

O'Hara didn't have much on which to spend the fifty dollars a month he was receiving from Uncle Sam. He wrote to Russell and proposed that the Mutual Investment Club raise its ten dollars a month dues to twenty dollars. Over several months, the other Mutual members noted that they, too, were finding few opportunities to spend their military pay. The doubling of contributions was almost unanimously enacted.

George Nicholson wasn't anything like Tom O'Hara imagined. Listening to Fred Russell describe this man for so long, at meetings and in his letters during the war, O'Hara had an almost mythical image of the man in his mind's eye. But now, seated across a luncheon table with him in a basement restaurant of a busy downtown Detroit hotel, Nicholson wasn't anything like O'Hara expected.

It was the spring of 1946. The war had ended the year before and the Mutual Investment Club had just held its first regular meeting since all the members had returned home from military service. This luncheon with Nicholson had come about after an idea brought up by Tom O'Hara was thoroughly shot down by the other members. O'Hara was excited by the great interest he had found during the war from everyone he talked to about the club. He saw great potential in expanding the investment club idea into a larger organization. When he proposed it to the other members, they disagreed. They liked things just as they were. They resumed their careers, reunited with their families and got on with their lives. No one wanted anything to do with the idea of converting the club into something bigger.

No one except Fred Russell.

As that meeting broke up, Russell asked the obviously disappointed Tom O'Hara to stay behind. "Tom," he confided after the others left, "I share your vision. I think we're really on to something here." Russell suggested the two of them have lunch with George Nicholson, whose ideas and investment principles served as the foundation for the club.

O'Hara expected Nicholson to be warm and gregarious.

Instead, he found a tall, bushy-eyebrowed, balding man who was quiet and detached. At thirty-eight, Nicholson was just seven years O'Hara's senior, but he looked much older. If O'Hara didn't know better, he'd have guessed Nicholson's age to be fifty. A big, broad-shouldered man who had played football under the legendary Fielding H. Yost at the University of Michigan, Nicholson was extremely formal for an ex-athlete, almost to the point of rudeness. He was polite enough, when first introduced to O'Hara but, after shaking hands with the eager young accountant, all but ignored him. O'Hara knew that Nicholson had gone on from the University of Michigan to graduate from the Harvard Business School and had a reputation in Detroit's financial community as a brilliant investment analyst. Still, O'Hara thought, that's no reason for Nicholson to ignore him. But that's just what he was doing.

Throughout the lunch, Nicholson discussed with Russell some investment situation back at the office. Whenever O'Hara tried to ask a question or bring up the idea of expanding the Mutual Investment Club, Nicholson paused for a brief moment, stared blankly at O'Hara, and then, without so much as a word, turned back to Russell and resumed the conversation as if O'Hara was not even there.

As the waiter, who obviously knew and deferred to Nicholson, began to clear away the dishes, O'Hara decided to try one last time. He waited for a lull in the conversation, then as cheerfully as he could, O'Hara jumped in and said how much he appreciated Nicholson's tutelage in guiding the Mutual Investment Club.

"It seems like all my life, from high school on, I thought everyone in the country ought to be a shareholder and when Fred got us all together it was a dream come true," he said. "Fred and I were talking and, well, we think that the ideas you have introduced us to in our investment club could lead to some sort of a bigger organization, an association."

There. He said it. It was out on the table. O'Hara waited for the great man to respond.

All he got was a grunt.

Then Nicholson turned back to Russell and, again, went right back to whatever they had been discussing.

That was it. A few minutes later, on the sidewalk outside, as Nicholson said a curt goodbye and started walking back to his office, Russell turned and whispered to O'Hara.

"That was a great luncheon. Really, Tom. Mr. Nicholson was impressed. You'll hear back from him soon."

Russell hurried after his boss, leaving a red-faced and thoroughly dejected O'Hara wondering whatever could possibly have given Russell that impression. As far as Tom O'Hara was concerned, the meeting had been a total bust. O'Hara figured it was the first and last time he would ever meet George Nicholson.

First impressions can't always be trusted. But O'Hara saw little reason to doubt his assessment of that first meeting. As one week, then two, and then a third passed with no further contact from either Russell or Nicholson, O'Hara concluded that his dream was just that.

Then George Nicholson called and invited him back to lunch at the same restaurant.

"I want to talk about building our club into a nationwide investment education project," he said.

O'Hara's spirits soared.

This time, O'Hara found George Nicholson as intensely focused on the investment club idea with him as he had been with whatever investment problem he and Russell had discussed three weeks before.

Nicholson confided that when he had helped Russell form the Mutual Investment Club he was beginning an experiment. Ever since he had run across investment clubs in Boston during his college days, Nicholson said, he had wondered if they could not be made into classrooms where individuals learned investment principles and practiced applying them with small amounts of money while they developed their skills and the confidence to experiment with larger sums of money. Investment clubs, Nicholson said, could become classrooms for mass-producing educated investors.

"When Fred came to me years ago to get advice on how a young man can accumulate enough money to start his own business, I decided right then and there to try out my idea," Nicholson explained. "If the young men Fred recruited would try applying my theories and actually develop individual investment skills in their club, I'd know this was a viable plan."

Nicholson said he was pleased with what O'Hara and the other members had done. He unfolded a neatly typewritten paper. "You boys have developed a little investment skill," he said approvingly. "You've learned how to select promising stocks and have accumulated a nice little portfolio." Nicholson showed that club members had invested a total of $5,080.

"It is now worth $9,844," said Nicholson. "You have not quite reached the goal of doubling in five years. But then, we had a World War to contend with, didn't we?"

Nicholson clearly believed the Mutual Investment Club proved his theory. He could now use it as an example to train investors on how to establish and implement other investment clubs.

O'Hara was thrilled. This was exactly what he wanted to do. His mind raced. He saw unlimited possibilities.

O'Hara's enthusiasm was short-lived. No sooner had Nicholson started creating visions about what could be than he announced that the time was not yet right. One investment club was not enough of an example. "We need more clubs," he said, "more examples that prove this concept really works."

However he had a surprise for O'Hara. The Mutual Investment Club was not the only organization Nicholson had helped form. Two other investment clubs were starting.

"I want another year or two to see how they perform," he said. "And I want to make more people aware of clubs as a tool for teaching and training investors. In the meantime, though, we should think about ways to start and build an organization that can provide impetus and strength to the new idea."

We.

Nicholson said we. He was including Tom O'Hara in his plans.

Though neither had a name for what was hatched at that meeting, that conversation was the seminal event that would lead to the National Association of Investment Clubs.

The details, the plan, the direction, the organization of it all would be hammered out and revised and strategized in a series of luncheons over the next four years. Besides the noontime sessions, there were literally hundreds of telephone conversations and meetings between the two in Nicholson's downtown Detroit office.

Methodically, Nicholson laid it all out. First, they would form a Trust.

He explained that he had seen a number of volunteer organizations over the years become involved in the turmoil of personal politics. He strongly felt that whatever organization he and O'Hara formed should have a solid Trust, or business unit, at its top, which would concentrate on building the association and not be subject to political pressures from individual members or clubs.

"Practically," he explained, "we know by experience that whenever you have people you have the politics of ambition and personal interest. That's just human nature."

To avoid those problems, he suggested the Trust form another organization with the directors elected by the membership. The Trust would operate the business free from political pressure from the members. The corporation set up by the Trust would have Directors elected by the membership. This corporation would then absorb the day-to-day contacts with the membership and all personal conflicts which otherwise might keep the Trustees from running the business of the organization. This group would maintain contact with all members, ensuring that their needs and desires would be known to both this group of leaders, and ultimately to the Trustees.

Nicholson had it all figured out, and as he met and planned with his new mentor over those four years from 1946 to 1949, Tom O'Hara marveled at Nicholson's management acumen.

The association would be a not-for-profit group, dependent on volunteers. Nicholson even drew up a national organizational chart.

All they needed were some members.

The original members recruited. Tom O'Hara brought in several new members. One of his most important recruits turned out to be Lewis Rockwell, an old college buddy. Tom and "Lew," as everyone called the jovial, quick-witted Detroit attorney, had been fraternity brothers at Wayne State University. During the war, they exchanged letters as they crisscrossed the globe. Rockwell was in Normandy and witnessed D-Day from the beach. Letters from O'Hara were in the pack he carried with him throughout that long, bloody campaign. In those letters, O'Hara mentioned several times that he was in an investment club that, amazingly enough, was functioning just fine with all its members fighting the war all over the world.

After the war, when Rockwell met O'Hara at a reunion of their Phi Gamma Chi fraternity, he couldn't wait to ask about the club.

"Why Lew," said O'Hara, after explaining how well the investments were doing, "why don't you join? You can put in any multiple of ten dollars a month. You'll hardly miss it and over time it really does add up, especially when we're all combining our contributions."

The conversation drew the attention of others and a small crowd gathered about. Before the night ended, two other reunited Phi Gamma Chi fraternity brothers, Bob Pryor and Bob Berger, joined Rockwell in asking to come into the club.

Fred Russell, meanwhile, was singing the Mutual Investment Club praises, too. He ran into an old friend from Wheaton College named Art Baske who had a good job with General Motors. He could afford the ten dollar a month dues. Russell brought him into the club.

George Nicholson watched all this expansion with quiet approval. As he saw the new men come and the enthusiasm build, he knew his idea to expand the investment club idea into an association would succeed.

In 1949, Nicholson decided it was time to introduce the world to his experiment.

Nicholson was well known and respected as a financial advisor and had extensive contacts in the media. He contacted Kenneth Thompson, the Financial Editor of the *Detroit Free Press*, and told him about the Mutual Investment Club of Detroit. Thompson was fascinated and ran a feature story about the club across two pages in the Sunday paper.

"Twelve Young Men Have Great Success With an Original Idea," read the banner headline in the feature section.

The story recounted the club's founding, how the members kept contributing even during the war and how they were beginning to amass impressive holdings by carefully following conservative and sound financial principles. At the time, the story noted, the Mutual Investment Club was worth $20,690. The reporter noted that one of the members, Fred Russell, had done so well that he had been able to withdraw three thousand dollars, enough to start a Howard Johnson's restaurant on Mack Avenue in the eastern Detroit suburb of Grosse Pointe Woods. The newspaper printed the names and work places of each of the members. None of them had ever had their name in the newspaper before, and all Sunday afternoon they basked in the limelight as they received calls from family and friends complimenting them on the article.

Little did they know what would happen on Monday.

Tom O'Hara was the manager of the Payroll Department of the Detroit Board of Education. When he arrived at the office that morning, the receptionist greeted him with a quick scowl.

"The Superintendent wants to see you in his office right away," she said, her tone formal, if not icy.

O'Hara rapped on the Superintendent's door and stepped inside.

Before he could even say good morning, the Superintendent let loose.

"O'Hara," he barked, "have you gone to work for a broker?"

Tom O'Hara was clueless. But before he could respond, the Superintendent continued.

"What have you got going on? Our switchboard is tied up with people calling you about stock."

For a moment, O'Hara was even more puzzled. Then he remembered the story in the Sunday edition of the newspaper and explained. The story had listed his name and job location. Readers were obviously looking it up and calling for more information.

The Superintendent looked relieved, but suspicious. "What you do in your personal time, O'Hara, is your own concern. But see to it that this stock thing does not intrude upon your work time."

Sheepishly, O'Hara agreed to the demand and retreated to his own office. He spent much of the rest of the day giving people his home phone number or promising to call them back in the evening.

It was the same with other club members. The public was fascinated by the article in the *Detroit Free Press* and wanted more information. Over six hundred people picked up the telephone and called the various members of the Mutual Investment Club. About half of the callers said that the idea of an investment club was not original at all and that they had been in investment clubs, too.

Some of those callers offered up some strongly-worded advice for the Mutual members: Get out quick, while they were still ahead! They recounted long, involved and sad stories about how they had lost their shirts by investing in stocks.

But that advice to get out was countermanded by the other half of the callers with investment club experience. They told the members to keep on investing for the rest of their lives. It was paying off for them, they said, and they were sure it would for the Mutual investors.

The response to the newspaper publicity was phenomenal and at the next meeting of the Mutual Investment Club little else was discussed.

The first thing the members addressed was the six hundred names. What were they to do with them?

"We need to learn from them," O'Hara said. "There's a wealth of wisdom they can provide us."

The club decided to send out a survey to the six hundred people who had called or written the individual members, hoping to learn why half the people did well and half failed. As the questionnaires came back, they quickly pointed to some key factors.

The clubs that didn't succeed followed an amazingly similar pattern. They had no system, no plan or policies to determine what was a good investment and what was not. There was no disciplne, either, nor any educational efforts to learn about the market. They simply started to invest when the market was going up. As their stocks went up in value, they sold them and put the proceeds in other stocks. As they continued, they bought more speculative and poorer quality stocks. When the market started its decline, their poor-quality stocks nose-dived. They took their losses and resolved never to invest again. It was sad and predictable.

It was just as George Nicholson had told the Mutual Investment Club when he stressed the importance of following his three principles of sound investment and warned what would happen if the principles were ignored.

However, the returned surveys revealed the successful groups also had shared characteristics. They followed one or more of the three things George had advised O'Hara and his friends to do. The successful clubs tried not to guess which way the market was going to move. They invested every month. They reinvested their earnings. And, perhaps most importantly, they studied the market and tried to learn how to pick stocks that would grow in value and thus one day sell at higher prices.

Digesting the information from the surveys took several months. The *Detroit Free Press* article had appeared in the fall of 1949. By the summer of 1950, as O'Hara and Russell poured over the results with Nicholson, they knew what needed to be done.

The questionnaires overwhelmingly showed that a lot of the former members of the clubs that failed wished they could start over. They expressed frustration in not knowing exactly where they went wrong and a longing to learn how to do it right.

On the other hand, members of the successful clubs were excited to share their experiences and anxious to learn how others were doing.

The result of the surveys and the follow-up calls that the Mutual Investment Cub had with many people over many months was that hundreds of people who were interested in investing in a group setting were enthusiastically talking to each other.

It was now abundantly clear that there was a need for an organization that would give new and existing clubs guidance and help them along the road to success.

"It's time," Nicholson told O'Hara. "We're ready to get this going."

The other two clubs that Nicholson had been instrumental in forming were also doing well, he explained. Nicholson brought out of a meticulously-labeled manila folder the handwritten notes he had scribbled out over those many lunches with O'Hara about setting up a Trust to administer the association.

"Call your lawyer friend," he told O'Hara. "Let's do it."

Lew Rockwell met with Tom O'Hara in the cafeteria of the Detroit Engineering Society on Woodward Avenue, right across the street from O'Hara's office with the Detroit Board of Education. He handed over Nicholson's notes.

"We have three clubs operating in Detroit right now," explained O'Hara as they ate their lunches in the marbled dining hall of the Society. "The idea is to start the Trust with twelve Trustees from those three clubs and call an organizing convention."

On August 28, 1951, Rockwell's Trust Agreement was ready to be signed and the representatives of the three clubs met for the first time.

The Mutual Investment Club of Detroit had done the organizing and the recruiting and ended up with the most significant representation. Besides O'Hara, Rockwell and Russell, members Dr. Justin H. Dunmire, James D. Youd, Robert L. Pryor, Arthur F. Baske, Robert A. Burger, George E. Palmer and Leo H. Jacobson became Trustees.

The second club was called the One Hundred Ten Club, from the city of Ann Arbor, just west of Detroit in Washtenaw County. It got its name from the fact that at its first meeting its members deposited and invested $110 each, though ten dollars was the continuing monthly sum. For several years, it had the dubious distinction of being an illustration of the price paid when a club failed to follow NAIC's guiding principles. Nicholson had made it very clear that members of a club should invest a set sum of money regularly over a long period of time, not a large sum at one time. But because the members of the One Hundred Ten Club thought they could jumpstart the club with a larger initial contribution, they ignored Nicholson's advice. Unfortunately for the members of the One Hundred Ten Club, the stock market was at a high when the $110 were invested at the club's first meeting. The market then started a decline that lasted more than a year and the members waited a long time to see the value of the club equal their investment. In time, of course, scrupulously following the rest of the NAIC principles, it did quite well, but the members always cautioned new clubs to spread their investments over a lengthy period and not invest a large sum to begin with.

Signing on for the One Hundred Ten Club was Lawrence Ozment and Frederick N. McOmber.

The third club was called the Pontiac Investment Club, from the city of Pontiac just north of Detroit in Oakland County. It provided three representatives to the Board of Trustees — Vernon L. Schiller, Richard E. Dibner and Robert L. Boynton.

One by one, the document was passed around the room.

"The purpose of this Trust is to aid in the preserving and strengthening of democratic capitalism by educating people in the investment principles that have and are now being employed by the members of the Mutual Investment Club of Detroit, Michigan, the Pontiac Investment Club of Pontiac, Michigan and the One Hundred Ten Club of Ann Arbor, Michigan."

Solemnly, each man signed his name. Years later, several wished they had kept the pens they used. They all reached into their billfolds and extracted a single dollar, giving the Trust its first assets. All were volunteers. They came from every walk of life. And although strangers, they had much in common. All were capitalists who fiercely believed in the free economic system. All believed in their country and had a deep and sincere desire to help as many people as possible become successful investors. And all were unusually fortunate in that they had come under the tutelage of George A. Nicholson, Jr., whose gentle guidance proved that by following some fairly simple steps, the ordinary individual could learn to make relatively safe and profitable investments.

As the men signed the Trust agreement and shook hands and slapped backs they knew that something significant, something that would truly be good for the whole country, indeed the whole world, had been set in motion. But they also had a lot of questions. They had just formed an organization, an association for investment clubs. The Trust agreement designed by Nicholson, drawn up by Rockwell and just signed by the fifteen of them gave them an organizational plan for governing the association.

But now what? There were many questions that day. Just how would they develop the organization? Publicize it? How would it then help others start clubs, teach others to pick stocks, keep records, pay taxes and a dozen other things? To operate, the association needed funds. Until then, none of the clubs had given much thought to money. Officers and other volunteers bought supplies themselves and paid their bills as they went along. Collections were made at meetings from time to time. But now, if this association was going to take off and grow, something more formal would have to be devised. How could these Trustees persuade other clubs and investors to pay dues to the association?

There were lots of excited suggestions and considerable shoulder shrugging, but few immediate answers. Nicholson, in telephone calls, after-hour meetings in his downtown office and across many a luncheon table, repeatedly assured the new Trustees that all these details would work out in time. The important thing was, they had joined together.

It was happening.

The new Trustees set the organizing convention for Saturday, October 20, 1951 at the Rackham Building in Detroit.

O'Hara volunteered to send out invitations to the six hundred people who had responded to the *Detroit Free Press* story the year before. Frederick McOmber was in charge of the program and Robert Pryor was in charge of reservations. The day-long program and lunch carried a registration fee of $2.75. Membership in the new organization was priced at a dollar per club member.

Anxiously, O'Hara checked the mail each day as the date for the organizing convention drew near. No one knew what kind of a response to expect.

It was better than many expected. Sixty-five people registered and twelve clubs became Charter Members at the founding meeting. George Nicholson gave the keynote address.

As he stood before those first members in his trademark navy blue suit, the big balding man with the bushy eyebrows beamed. It was a dream come true and, inside, he was deeply satisfied. But he knew a long road lay ahead.

"The significance of our action today might not be known for many years," he said. "Quite possibly, it will turn out to be much ado about nothing. But any time a movement grows out of the grass roots of America, as this one has done, and secures the active participation of so many men and women of all ages and circumstances, it has, to say the least, the potential of wielding a vast influence... To be sure, it is no atom bomb, but it has, perhaps, a greater explosive power."

NAIC, he said, was a reality. At that time, NAIC stood for National Association of Investors Clubs. Later it would be changed, at the urging of members, to National Association of Investors Corporation. Nicholson's inspiring speech drew a standing ovation. He was so well received, in fact, that he would go on to deliver the keynote speech at forty-four following annual meetings.

At that meeting members elected the first Board of National NAIC Directors. They voted in Wagar Glas of the One Hundred Ten Club as Chairman. His vigorous leadership led to his re-election each year through October 1968.

Members elected Lewis Rockwell, who had drafted NAIC's Trust Agreement, President of the Board. They chose Haig Avedesian, as Vice President. Richard Dibner and Robert Stoetzer were also elected Vice Presidents. Betty Kaufmann became Secretary and James Youd, Treasurer. The other Directors were James Faucher, Ben Dickinson, Lyndon Kaufmann, John F. Anderson and George Woods.

These were the pioneers. The organization they formed a half century ago has since helped provide financial stability for countless families, enabling individuals to buy homes, send children to college, pay for weddings, give generously to churches and charities and live comfortably in retirement. It has directly led to the creation of hundreds of thousands of jobs. Its investment and influence has saved corporations from financial disaster, spurred research and development, brought about tremendous technological advancements, inspired the creation of new and fairer investment and tax laws and, in a very real sense, kept America strong.

Chapter Three: **Building a Dream**

"The great things in life cannot be bought"

Tom O'Hara said he really did want to get married. Very much so.

But first, he explained to Eleanor Urquhart, he had to pay for his car.

It didn't take O'Hara long after his return from the war to find his college sweetheart. He found her at church.

It was a Sunday night service and O'Hara was dragged along by his parents. He didn't like Sunday night services. He always went Sunday morning and figured that was enough. But his mother always urged him to come back to church with her on Sunday nights and finally, all out of excuses, he agreed.

Sometime during the second hymn, he turned around to see who was there. A couple of rows behind him, there she was with her brother. Prettier than ever. His heart flipped. Their eyes locked. She smiled.

That was it. He knew he was in love and this was the girl he wanted to spend the rest of his life with. Just like that.

Eleanor had the same job in the personnel department of the Detroit Oil Company where she had worked during college. She was delighted to see the handsome, blue-eyed O'Hara. Without missing a beat, they resumed their relationship right where they left off the night Eleanor's Mom suggested that they postpone their dating until Tom got through college and put his life on sound financial footing.

O'Hara had a good job now. A future. Eleanor had known, even back in school, that he was a good catch. He was a straight-A student, popular with everyone, a great tennis player, a leader in every college organization he joined. He was funny, too, fun to be with, gifted with a great sense of humor, even if he did talk about business all the time. He would be a good provider, Eleanor knew, responsible and disciplined with money.

Perhaps too disciplined.

He proposed around Christmastime in 1949. There was just one catch. That new 1948 Studebaker he was still buying. Until the car was completely paid for, he said, he couldn't get married. He didn't want to start a marriage in debt.

But Eleanor knew he loved her. And she loved him, too. What was a few more months?

In late April of 1950, Tom O'Hara made his last sixty-dollar payment on the green Studebaker.

They married on May 6, 1950, honeymooning on the exclusive Jekyll Island, just off the coast of Georgia, a resort favored by some of the richest, most exclusive families in America. The Jekyll Island Club was an incredibly luxurious place where people like the Rockefellers, Morgans and Vanderbilts enjoyed the beauty and seclusion of the Georgia seacoast.

For two weeks in May of 1950, the new Mr. and Mrs. Thomas O'Hara joined the elite. Besides making the car payments, O'Hara, it turned out, had been scrimping and saving for months to take his young bride to the honeymoon paradise.

The honeymoon was a delightful respite. When they returned to Detroit, moving into a modest colonial in Huntington Woods, just off Woodward Avenue, a couple of miles north of Detroit, George Nicholson was one of Tom's first callers.

They had work to do, he said.

George Nicholson, a man of boundless energy, worried there wouldn't be enough time to accomplish all he hoped to do in his lifetime. Going back in his family a half dozen generations, he said, no Nicholson man had lived past the age of seventy. Therefore, he explained when people puzzled at his intensity, he was particularly cognizant of time and his responsibility to make the most of it.

The tall, solidly-built Nicholson was an avid tennis player and exercised vigorously, a habit from his old football days. He played under the University of Michigan's legendary Fielding H. Yost, who drilled into his players that to be successful on the field you needed a strong defense and a long scoring play. Those were two principles that Nicholson carried with him off the field, too, using them to shape every aspect of his life. In financial matters, it meant protecting the investment at all costs, holding on to it despite the external pressure of the marketplace. And it meant growing that investment over the long haul by exploiting the openings and opportunities presented by the economy and world events.

On a personal level, his former coach's football advice meant taking care of himself. The grandson of a Lutheran minister, Nicholson first did so spiritually, reading the Bible each day and teaching it in Sunday School at Christ Church in Grosse Pointe.

And he took care of himself physically, too. Friends would joke about the alarms and timers he carried that sounded regularly during the day, signaling him that it was time to reach into a vest pocket and remove a pillbox for a vitamin or mineral supplement.

One time as a young girl, his daughter Beth saw him leaving the house with a box of chocolates.

"What are you going to do with the candy, Daddy?" she asked.

"Why, these are for my doctor," he explained, hazel eyes twinkling. "I give him a box every year when I have my annual examination. I want him to do a good job, you know."

Nicholson and his wife Elizabeth, who everyone called "Libby," had four children, Beth and three sons. Everyone, family, friends and business associates — marveled at his positive attitude. An avid student of politics, the economy and world affairs, he never spoke negatively about anything except communism. He had lived through the Great Depression, seen the evils of Hitler's fanaticism and watched the Cold War and the Korean War test the nation's resolve. He believed with all his heart that the American way of life, democratic capitalism, was the best hope for the world. He even wrote an editorial in one of the early editions of NAIC's *Better Investing* publication addressed to then-Russian dictator Nikita Khrushchev. "An Investment Club, Nikita?" Nicholson suggested that if the Russian leader really wanted to raise the standard of living for his people he would get rid of communism, embrace capitalism and, well...start an investment club.

He was serious.

He was a visionary. That's how everyone who spent even brief amounts of time with the man described him.

"The great things in life cannot be bought," he wrote. "The heart of our movement is democratic capitalism. This is far more than the widespread ownership of industry for it includes, as well, a flexible concept of capitalism and socialism and the concept of an increasing number of economically stable families.

"There can be little doubt that our concept of mass production can produce the highest standard of living. At the same time, there can be no questioning the fact that periods of economic adjustment must inevitably come and limited socialistic measures are necessary to preserve minimum living standards and provide economic security for those lowest on the economic scale. The pendulum swings from one extreme to the other with changing conditions; the fact that it is free to swing is perhaps the sole reason why our democracy has proved so pliable and enduring and survived even civil war."

Nicholson envisioned widespread ownership in business, just what NAIC provided through pooled investments, as the key to the production of economically stable families.

"Without widespread ownership, public apathy is likely to develop. Public apathy abroad has led to government ownership of big business, competition has given way to government monopoly and high cost inefficiency; government monopoly in the end has resulted in state control of the worker —- slavery."

"However," wrote Nicholson in those early days of NAIC, "economically stable families will give new meaning to what the free world can do."

Right after the Trust Agreement had been signed and the Association formed, O'Hara, Rockwell, Russell and others sent out newsletters and bulletins. Nicholson wrote parts of them, too. But because he worked for a brokerage firm and scrupulously wished to avoid even the hint of a conflict in interest lest any of his clients think he was recommending certain stocks for personal gain, he initially wrote under the pseudonym, "Saint Nick." His daughter Beth thought the moniker he chose was appropriate, because of his twinkling eyes.

They called the newsletter simply, *NEWS.* It consisted of a single mimeographed sheet. There wasn't much news at first. The first issue, Volume 1, Number 1, was published on September 10, 1951, six weeks before the convention. It said the *NEWS* would discuss and explain investment principles to help members develop their own investing skills. It promised investment information on specific companies and, someday, classes for club members on investing.

The bulletins, usually first handwritten by Trustees on yellow legal pads and then typewritten by secretaries borrowed from Rockwell and Nicholson and some of their wives, bore long and sometimes ponderous titles. Although they were initially sent out individually, eventually, they were all compiled in a single volume as an *"Investor's Manual"* and enthusiastically used as a start-up blueprint by many new clubs for years.

Bulletin I was titled *Suggested Points to Include In a New Club's By-laws.* It basically was a copy of the operating agreement of the Mutual Investment Club and it served as the starting point for dozens of new clubs.

Bulletin II was *A Suggested Investment Policy for the First Two*

Years of a New Investment Club. Art Baske, who wrote technical service bulletins for General Motors cars, made Nicholson's advice and the Mutual Investment Club's experiences understandable to the average reader. The bulletin suggested buying one stock a month during the first year. In the second year it recommended a careful re-study of the twelve stocks with emphasis on the sales growth, earnings per share growth and on margins — not on the price of the stock. When those figures were up but the price was down, NAIC urged more purchases of those stocks. Or if the price of one or two stocks rose too high, they recommended a sale.

O'Hara wrote *Bulletin III, Record Keeping For an Investment Club,* which, at four pages and with accompanying illustrations, became the longest of them all. One of the first problems new clubs faced was how to keep records so that members could have different amounts invested, skip payments, make extra payments or draw out part of their investment and still share all gains and losses equitably. The Mutual Investment Club had solved the difficulties years before by applying the same type of accounting procedures used by pension funds. O'Hara produced a step-by-step reproduction of the monthly records kept by Mutual's treasurer each month.

Bulletin IV, Company Analysis Procedure, was just two pages long and contained instructions for clubs to calculate each member's share of taxable income. O'Hara used part of a lunch hour from his Board of Education job to visit the Detroit office of the Internal Revenue Service to make sure the bulletin was advising members correctly.

Bulletin V, Check List for Company Study, had all the basic elements that later went into NAIC's Stock Selection Guide. Yet it overwhelmed many of the initial readers. Nicholson thought the instructions were clearly stated and easily understandable, but the feedback the other directors received was not encouraging. Many said they were frustrated and thought that stock study was simply too complicated for the average person. While most clubs eventually found at least one person willing to read the suggestions and put the earning and growth figures down as suggested in Nicholson's "Check List," it became readily apparent that NAIC truly did need to undertake a massive educational project if the clubs were going to become self sufficient and thrive.

A final *Bulletin* was created to handle the paperwork confusion. At the time, few brokerage firms had experience with clubs or investor partnerships. And for customers, many who remembered hearing about brokers going bankrupt after the big crash of '29, the idea of letting brokers hold their securities for them was an unsettling notion. Most customers wanted their investment certificates in their own hands, not those of a broker. Clubs needed an agreement form they could give their broker that outlined the way they wanted their account handled. Brokers wanted a uniform agreement to be used by all clubs to solve this problem. Nicholson devised a special standardized form that was published as NAIC *Bulletin No. VI.*

But as nice as the forms and bulletins were, the fact was that in the early fifties no one at NAIC, other than Nicholson, had any more experience picking stocks than they had picked up from their own investment clubs. It was up to Nicholson to educate his own directors first so they could educate the new members in turn.

As the mail came in and new clubs formed, he suggested the new Association had three distinct responsibilities. He wrote them down and sent them around to the other board members.

1. NAIC's main job would be teaching individuals sound investment principles and how to apply them.
2. NAIC needed to build its membership both to have people teach and to provide income to finance its operations.
3. To attract and hold members, NAIC needed to develop services that would be valuable to its members.

On the first point, everyone agreed. They were already well on their way to doing that, passing along information through the new publications and in the regular meetings of the individual clubs. But on the other two, building a financially supportive membership and developing services, they clearly needed to do a lot of work.

George Nicholson set out to do that with a lot of traveling.

Nicholson worked for the firm of Watling, Lerchen & Co., which was one of Michigan's top quality brokerage firms. It had a loose association with a number of similar brokerage houses scattered around the country. These firms had frequent meetings where their executives exchanged ideas and Nicholson took every opportunity to attend. His pitch was simple. It was in the financial interest of security salesmen to encourage their clients to start investment clubs. That way, the salesmen could build radiation business from the individual members of those clubs. As the clients experienced success through the investment club, Nicholson reasoned, they'd eventually want to open up personal accounts for themselves. And as those personal accounts grew, relatives and friends would become interested. All this would translate into increased commissions to the security salesmen.

It was like a light bulb going on all over the country. Until Nicholson pointed out the benefits for the broker, most security salesmen didn't think much of investment clubs. The typical ten dollars a month paid in by the fifteen or sixteen people who formed the average club, was chicken feed to them. Besides, there was a tremendous amount of paperwork. Thus, many brokers refused to take investment club business or greatly discouraged it. Then Nicholson showed them how nothing breeds success like success and that the relationships brokers formed with individuals through clubs translated into all that radiation business. It seemed like everyone wanted to talk to George Nicholson. He soon found large hunks of his day taken up in telephone calls with other brokers eager to form investment clubs.

One of the men Nicholson enthralled was Alex Carroll, who was in charge of developing salesmen for the Indianapolis office of the Thomson McKinnon brokerage house. A charismatic and energetic salesman, Carroll became an evangelist for Nicholson's investment club ideas, training other brokers and security salesmen throughout the Midwest in the art of dealing with investment clubs. He even persuaded the University in Indianapolis to sponsor several investment conferences dealing with the ins and outs of investment clubs.

James C. Barnes was one of the young salesmen Carroll mentored. Barnes worked out of Thomson McKinnon's South Bend office and one day in the mid-fifties addressed an investment class at the local YMCA. It was a standard NAIC pitch, in which Barnes suggested investment clubs as a way that average people could get started in investing without much knowledge or money.

The audience listened politely but not particularly inspired. Except for one person. A woman. The lone woman in the YMCA audience. Her name was Mrs. Louis N. Rugge and she was there that day, she explained to Barnes after the session, only because her husband had insisted she attend.

"He told me that for the first time in his life he was making good money and putting most of it into stocks," Mrs. Rugge explained. "Then he pointed out that the mortality statistics indicate that I will be around a long time after he is gone. Since he was putting his money in stock he figured I had better learn about investing, because the odds are I will end up looking after the stock when he dies."

Mrs. Rugge turned out to be a star pupil. She signed up for the local club organized by Barnes and, over several months, found that by scrupulously following the NAIC suggestions, she was indeed able to considerably grow her investments. With great satisfaction and peace of mind about her financial future, she thanked Barnes and said that she owed her success to him. He thanked her and felt good that he was helping people. Little did the young broker realize what good fortune was about to befall him because of his enthusiastic student.

Barnes didn't realize that Mrs. Rugge was President of the South Bend Federation of Women's Clubs. In that role, almost every day, she visited and addressed a different ladies' club throughout northern Indiana. Her audiences were eager to learn about personal finance management and, in just about every talk she gave, she told of the success she was experiencing through her investment club.

"Most of you will be widows," she told her audiences. "Now is the time to learn how to be financially independent."

The women responded with great interest, inevitably asking what broker handled her investment club. Why, Jim Barnes, she said, passing out his business cards to eagerly outstretched hands.

Barnes soon oversaw a booming business. In a little over a year's time, he was handling two hundred investment clubs. Soon, he netted over one hundred thousand dollars a year, which, in the mid-fifties, was a very handsome income. With so much new business, Barnes quickly earned a reputation as being the investment club expert of the brokerage business. In a few years he became a full partner in the firm and moved to New York, where he headed the training of all of Thomson McKinnon's new salesmen across the country. The first thing Barnes did was to make sure that handling investment clubs became a part of everyone's training at that firm.

Despite the encouraging growth, NAIC had a significant problem. The association had no money. The bank balance at the end of the month was rarely over one hundred dollars.

The Board of Trustees decided to ask for financial support from corporate America. It was during the height of the Cold War. The Korean conflict was still very much in the news and the slogan "Better Red than Dead" was emerging on college campuses. As the Association saw it, and George Nicholson concurred, what was ultimately at stake in the titanic philosophical clash between communism and capitalism was the American free market system and the economic viability of the United States. If the forces from the far left of the political spectrum had their way, Nicholson counseled, there would be no American stock market twenty years in the future. The Association saw itself as a lynchpin for democracy. By educating consumers about the opportunities provided by share ownership in corporations, they were directly working for America. Thus, it was in the direct interest of corporate America to support the NAIC. The Association's efforts to get millions of new investors to put ten dollars a month away for stock purchases would supply the capital needed to keep business growing forever.

With confidence born of naïve idealism, the trustees looked to Tom O'Hara. They appointed him the Association's chief fundraiser, and his first assignment was to go to New York.

There were only two problems. Tom O'Hara had no experience as a fundraiser. That didn't seem to bother any of the trustees because they didn't either. Besides, everybody liked Tom O'Hara and he knew NAIC better than anyone.

The second problem was their NAIC treasury held no money to finance such a trip.

Didn't O'Hara have some vacation time coming from the school board, someone asked?

He did.

Wouldn't New York be a wonderful place for the O'Hara family to take a vacation, someone else suggested?

"Sure," said Tom. And off he went in the family station wagon with Eleanor and two boys, seven and nine years old. O'Hara was optimistic. And firmly convinced NAIC was a worthy cause and should be warmly embraced by everyone interested in strengthening capitalism.

He selected two places in New York to make his first fundraising calls — the Alfred P. Sloan Foundation and the New York Stock Exchange.

O'Hara thought his Detroit connections would be a foot in the door at the Sloan Foundation, a philanthropic nonprofit institution established in 1934 by Alfred Pritchard Sloan, Jr., former President and Chief Executive Officer of General Motors Corporation. He couldn't have been more wrong. He did get in the office, but he got nowhere fast. After introducing himself and explaining what the Association was, he got no further than suggesting that perhaps the foundation would see it worthwhile to help underwrite some of NAIC's expenses.

"I'm so sorry sir," said a polite, but obviously busy man, who eventually agreed to see O'Hara after an hour's wait in the reception area, "but the Foundation has a very precise list of objectives that must be met by the organizations we support. It is my opinion it would be difficult, if not impossible, to fit your request into that list."

With that, Tom O'Hara found himself with a free afternoon to take Eleanor and the boys sightseeing in Manhattan.

The next day, he moved on to the New York Stock Exchange. O'Hara was confident that the Exchange was just waiting for an organization like NAIC. After all, the organization offered the potential to create millions of new customers for the securities industry.

This time, O'Hara was ushered into the office of a very personable vice-president of the exchange whose name was given so fast that O'Hara never did get it. Later, he would learn that there were lots of vice presidents on the New York Stock Exchange and there were lots of supplicants like O'Hara who were convinced that they deserved support.

The man listened very carefully to his request. He seemed, unlike the man from the Sloan Foundation, to have all the time in the world. O'Hara pleaded his case, passionately, telling of George Nicholson, Fred Russell, the Mutual Investment Club, all the newspaper coverage and the hundreds of members and new investment clubs. When he finished, he sat back in his chair.

The Vice President smiled. Warmly. He said how good it was to learn of such a group as the NAIC because, indeed, the Exchange and the securities industry as a whole welcomed new customers.

But there was one problem, said the man from the New York Stock Exchange.

"You see," he said, still smiling, "the industry and the Exchange are not really equipped to handle a large number of very small investors."

The vice president was very nice. But very clear.

"In my opinion," he said, "it is extremely unlikely that your Association will receive any funds from the securities industry. The reality is that the business offices of large firms consider an investment club more of a nuisance than an asset."

He stood up and shook O'Hara's hand. As O'Hara turned to leave, the man offered a suggestion. "Since you are from Detroit, perhaps you could take your request to the auto companies," he said.

O'Hara was crestfallen. His confidence had burst like a popped balloon. He decided not to try any more meetings with Manhattan's financial elite. The rest of that trip was all vacation for the O'Hara family, though several times Eleanor, noticing a sad and faraway look in her husband's eyes, reached over to pat his hand. "It will be all right, Tom," she said. "Don't give up. This will all work out. Just you wait and see."

He smiled back. "Sure honey, you're right," he said. But he wasn't so sure.

She didn't say anything but, if the truth were told, neither was she.

Back in Detroit, O'Hara decided to make one last effort. Following the advice from the Stock Exchange vice president, he sent a letter requesting a meeting with Charles E. Wilson, President of General Motors. To O'Hara's surprise, Wilson agreed and O'Hara soon found himself on the executive floor of the General Motors Building in midtown Detroit. Wilson, who was soon to become U.S. Secretary of Defense under President Dwight D. Eisenhower and known for the saying "what's good for GM is good for the country," couldn't have been a more ebullient and congenial host.

He seemed genuinely interested in O'Hara's recitation of NAIC and its goal to create millions of educated investors who would help undergird American businesses, even General Motors. However, when O'Hara inquired about whether GM would help finance the Association, Wilson quickly cut the conversation off with a chuckle. He told O'Hara that no matter how NAIC described itself, many businessmen, apparently including himself, would think that NAIC was just a clever promotional idea thought up by the securities industry, in hopes of getting someone else to pay the costs.

Wilson and GM weren't interested.

When NAIC Trustees met again, O'Hara was clearly discouraged. He grimly recounted the reactions to his fundraising pleas in New York and at the General Motors Building. O'Hara had no new ideas to offer.

There were few questions and a lot of head shaking. Disillusionment hung heavy.

Then one of the Trustees, Richard Dibner, snapped them all out of it.

"We've been running on the wrong track," said Dibner. "We've been looking for someone to do this for us. And that's all wrong. If we are to succeed, we have to run this as a business. That means we need to develop our own income and not depend upon anyone."

He had a proposal. NAIC had been selling its material to help a new club get started for one dollar. Dibner said that was too cheap. "Let's charge ten dollars for the material and then give a credit slip with it for the first ten dollar's worth of club dues," he suggested.

Why hadn't someone thought of it before? To Tom O'Hara and the other Trustees, it made tremendous sense.

Immediately, the Trustees pounced on the idea. They changed club dues from a dollar per member to ten dollars for the club and then an additional dollar for each member. Dibner's idea worked virtually overnight. The person who started a new investment club first bought the starting materials for ten dollars. When the club was underway and joined NAIC, the club collected the full dues from all the members and repaid the ten dollars to the member who had first bought the material. In turn, that person used the ten dollar credit slip for the initial club dues.

Until that restructuring in the dues and fees, only about one in twenty of the groups that had paid a dollar for the start-up materials actually joined NAIC. With Dibner's proposal in place, it was if the Association had hired fulltime organizers. The person who had personally invested ten dollars for the material was highly motivated to persuade the group to join. That way, the organizer got the ten dollars back.

Membership and the NAIC treasury surged together under the new procedures. From that time on, NAIC was totally self-supporting. But only because all its officers and workers were volunteers.

Besides singing the glories of investment clubs throughout his industry, George Nicholson was always on the lookout for ways to get the investment club story to the general public.

At a broker's conference that Nicholson addressed out east one day, he was pleased to find in the audience an editor from the prestigious *Kiplinger* financial magazine. Nicholson pulled the man aside and persuaded him to do a feature about investment clubs. It wasn't a huge audience but because the magazine was distributed nationally, it had a wide readership. Over four hundred *Kiplinger* readers wrote to NAIC asking for information about investment clubs.

Nicholson also did his own writing. As a Harvard Business School graduate, he published a story on "Investment Clubs and Investment Education" in the *Harvard Business School Bulletin* Winter 1953 issue. It described investment clubs as a classroom for beginning investors, helping individuals accumulate capital, thus providing capital for new ventures and working to create a nation of capitalists. It was pure Nicholson. And, while the *Harvard Business School Bulletin* was not widely read back then, those who did subscribe tended to be the movers and shakers of the financial community. So while Nicholson's Harvard story did not result in many letters to NAIC, it did get the attention of a number of editors from other, larger publications. Many quickly assigned their staff reporters to "this new investment club trend."

Thus, in January 1955, *Newsweek* magazine ran a feature story based largely on Nicholson's writing for his alma mater. At the end of the story, Newsweek printed NAIC's address as a source for more information about investment clubs. The location *Newsweek* printed, though, was actually the Detroit law office of Lew Rockwell, who volunteered his address to NAIC so it would appear to be more substantial than a group that operated out of Tom O'Hara's kitchen in suburban Huntington Woods.

O'Hara was working for the Detroit Board of Education at the time, running the Payroll Department. He also had a growing family. He and Eleanor had a son, Thomas Jr., born the same year NAIC was formed, in 1951. Eighteen months later, in 1953, came another boy, Robert. The two boys would play at their father's feet in the evenings as he processed the NAIC mail. He brought it home with him each night. During his lunch hour or after work, he stoped by Rockwell's office to pick it up. On a normal day, fifteen to twenty letters arrived. Not bad, they figured.

After the *Newsweek* story, that dramatically changed.

The first couple of days after the magazine hit the stands, the letters came in large bundles fastened with string or thick rubber bands. Then entire sacks of mail with hundreds of letters arrived. This happened every day for weeks. Instead of taking the bus to work as he usually did, O'Hara had to drive the family car to work to carry the mail home. More than five thousand letters poured in within a few short weeks all asking for investment club information.

It all fell upon Tom O'Hara. His young family quickly devised a system. The two O'Hara boys opened the letters. They were only four and five-years-old at the time, but they soon became experts at slitting envelopes, unfolding letters and stapling them to the envelopes. With good-natured joking and lots of cookies as rewards, the family processed the mail.

Most letter writers just wanted information about how to start a club. Quickly, Tom created a form letter. However, many others, too many to keep up, needed individual replies. O'Hara dictated the answers to Eleanor at night. The next day, while Tom was at the Board of Education, after she had taken care of little Tommy and Bobby, Eleanor sat at a typewriter and typed up her husband's replies.

It became impossible for Eleanor to keep up with the mail. The Association's secretary, Robert Pryor, headed up the business side of the styling department at the Ford Motor Company. He volunteered his secretary for a time, but even that wasn't enough. Eventually, O'Hara found a woman who agreed to do the letters at home at an affordable hourly rate and, over a couple of months, the pile was finally reduced to a manageable size.

Soon it became apparent that NAIC needed an office of its own. As good-natured as Rockwell was, the amount of NAIC mail and phone calls coming into his law office each day interfered with his own business.

The space next to Rockwell in Detroit's National Bank Building became available and the NAIC Trustees nervously voted, on March 1, 1956, to put the Association on the line for monthly rent and telephone charges. They hired George Nicholson's son, Edwin, at a minimum wage to staff the new, official NAIC office. For the weary volunteers this seemed like a giant step forward. Actually, they all continued to work just as hard as ever. It was just that now they had a fixed place to pick up and deliver their assignments. Ed Nicholson eagerly attacked the work, organizing it into piles for the volunteers and handling all the requests for information and materials.

Meanwhile, George Nicholson watched over all of this with great satisfaction, but a growing sense of urgency. NAIC was a mission to George Nicholson. As he saw all the mail and the fervent interest, he was driven with a renewed passion to spread the gospel of financially secure families.

And so, he drove Tom O'Hara. He drove him nuts.

Sometimes he'd call him three or four times a day at work. Another couple of times at home after work. Nicholson had a new idea every hour.

"George, you just spent five minutes laying out for me another project that will take six months," a weary O'Hara remembered protesting one time.

"Well, Tom, we are in this for the long haul," he replied.

The ideas were good. That was the problem, O'Hara realized. Nicholson thought O'Hara should arrange meetings with influential people. They should write articles and training materials for club members. Organizational ideas. Publicity campaigns. Seminars and strategy sessions. On and on.

The problem was, there wasn't enough time in the day to do all that needed to be done. O'Hara had two jobs, the salaried job at the School Board, which he found increasingly less satisfying, and the NAIC volunteer job, which paid nothing but satisfaction and took increasingly longer parts of his day. And night. And weekends.

O'Hara brought so much work home from NAIC that there wasn't room in the kitchen anymore. By the mid-fifties, piles and boxes of mail and NAIC literature spread out throughout the house, in closets, the living room, dining room, even their bedroom. To solve the space crunch, O'Hara constructed a small office above the garage but after a couple of years, it too, was bursting with boxes of paperwork.

Finally Eleanor O'Hara put her foot down. She wasn't worried about the mess. Her husband really was a neat man. He liked order. She was worried about the physical toll all the extra work was taking on him.

"One night in early January, 1958, after the kids had gone to sleep and he had climbed up over the garage to the office he set up to handle his NAIC work, she gave him an ultimatium. "Tom," she said, "you can't keep working like this. It's wearing you out. You have two choices. Either quit the School Board or quit the Association. You can't keep doing both."

O'Hara had learned long ago to listen to his wife. He put down whatever letter he was looking at and rubbed his bloodshot eyes. He looked at his wife, smiling at him warmly and gently through her own tired eyes. He could see the extra work was also taking its toll on Eleanor, who pitched in and helped every night. Even the little O'Hara boys helped their parents by opening and stapling the mail.

Tom O'Hara was doing more work than any one man could do, if that man expected to stay healthy and strong. But to quit the School

Board job? It represented security. It paid well. He knew he could work there until retirement. To give all that up for a barely organized, non-profit Association frightened him. If he was a single man, O'Hara thought, without a family to support, that would be one thing. But he had to think of Eleanor and the boys.

So what if he found little joy in the School Board. He remembered those men he passed as a boy during the Depression. He should thank God for the job he had, boring as it may be.

"It's just that this has grown so fast," he said, sweeping his hand at the piles of unanswered mail. "I always hoped, of course, that the Association would take off. And maybe at the back of my mind I pictured myself doing this full-time. But this has overwhelmed us all. I'm sorry."

Eleanor interrupted him. "Tom, I'm not saying you have to give the Association up. You can do it full-time. But you can't do it and the School Board. Quit the Board, I don't care. Or quit the Association if you feel you must do that. You just can't keep working at this pace, seven days a week, sixteen hours a day."

"But, the Association is not a sure thing. If the economy hits hard times, income could dry up overnight. It would be too unstable. How secure could our future be? I can't risk that for you and the boys."

"Talk to George," she said. "Talk to George. Just promise me, you'll do something about this. And soon. I'm too young to be a widow."

After Eleanor went back to the house, he sat at his little desk above the garage and thought hard about what his wife had said. There was no arguing with her. NAIC had gotten out of control. It consumed him. Across the country, new clubs jumped on board every day. There were nearly fifteen hundred of them by the spring of 1958 and almost 25,000 individual members. Letters and informational requests from new members crammed his desk. His heart quickened at the thought of quitting his accountant's job at the Board of Education and making NAIC his life's work.

There was no disputing NAIC's success. O'Hara had the growth statistics on his desktop. From twelve clubs in 1951, NAIC had grown to fifty-nine clubs with total assets of $170,000 by the start of 1953. Eight months later, it had 101 member clubs. Although

O'Hara's initial approach to the New York Stock Exchange did not arouse much enthusiasm, NAIC received its first major recognition by the securities industry when Edward T. McCormick, the dynamic President of the rival American Stock Exchange addressed NAIC's Third National Convention. In 1955, there was the huge growth spurt unleashed by Nicholson's *Harvard Business Review* article and the *Newsweek* story. So many people were interested in the Association that in August 1955, the original mimeographed publication simply called *NEWS* was renamed the *Bulletin* and commercially printed, complete with profitable full-page ads from the brokerage firm of Thompson & McKinnon and Poor's Investment Advisory Service.

That very same fall, all but erasing the bad memory of O'Hara's disastrous first trip to New York, Keith Funston, Chairman of the New York Stock Exchange, made a pilgrimage west to address the National Convention. The Exchange was even distributing NAIC promotional materials. Across the country, nearly a hundred newspapers were running a weekly investment column produced by NAIC called "Today's Investor." As a result, new and vibrant NAIC chapters opened in Chicago, Philadelphia and other big cities. There was even an NAIC chapter in Canada with more than a hundred clubs of its own. As O'Hara sat in his garage office on that cold winter's night in 1958, he realized that, with some 2,800 member clubs in two countries, NAIC had truly become a major player in the investment world.

One of the reports on his desk caught his eye and made him chuckle. It was from a group called the Money Bag Investment Club and the paper they had sent O'Hara detailed a new way they devised to do the NAIC stock selection guide. By using a special program developed on something called the Royal McBee LGP-30 Electronic Computer, the club said, a study could be completed in as little as five minutes. The club offered a copy of the program to anyone who had access to a Royal McBee Computer. Whatever that was. O'Hara didn't understand these new-fangled electronic machines, but he did understand the enthusiasm in that report from the Money Bag Club. NAIC was changing lives. The club's carefully taught principles of selecting stocks, whether done by pencil and paper as originally devised or on these new electronic contraptions, worked. Individual investors, average, everyday people, were becoming financially secure through the efforts of NAIC.

Many stories poured into the Association illustrating the wisdom of long-term investing and what NAIC was encouraging. O'Hara kept many on his desk or in his briefcase or in neat files stuck away in cabinets. One of the most heartwarming he had was a letter from A. L. Brooks of Port Nachez, Texas, who reported he had started his first investment club in 1898 in Corsicana, Texas. Brooks said he was one of twelve in the club. He put five dollars a month out of his $35 salary into his club, money, he said, he earned from working twelve to sixteen hours a day, seven days a week around the pecan farms and oil fields of Navarro County, an hour's drive south of Dallas. That was his first investment club and over the better part of two decades, he said, he managed to save a thousand dollars.

In 1923, Brooks said, he organized another club known as the First National Company. It, too, was successful. So successful that Brooks became a banker by occupation. By 1950, his First National investment club's net worth had grown larger than the capital of his bank. Brooks said that in 1955, after retiring from the banking business, he organized his third club at age 73.

NAIC's principles worked. There were scores of other letters just as inspirational.

NAIC had become a movement, O'Hara realized.

Maybe his dream wasn't so farfetched after all. He looked again at the charts, reports, growth statistics, and letters that were neatly stacked on his garage desktop. There was no disputing it. He had been so busy trying to keep his head above water that he missed the ocean that had formed all around him.

NAIC was vibrant and growing and, if he didn't quit his job with the School Board and devote all his activities to it, it would, as his wife warned, soon kill him.

Unless he quit NAIC, and stayed with the School Board.

He realized with a sigh, if he did that, if he walked away from his dream, his heart would break.

He had no choice.

Chapter Four: **On the Road**

To say it was easy wouldn't be accurate. But then again, exchanging the security of a government job for the excitement of working for an all-volunteer organization that totally depended on dues for income wasn't nearly as difficult as Tom O'Hara expected, either.

Eleanor totally supported his decision. She was relieved, knowing that Tom would be happier and healthier with just one job, no matter how tenuous that job appeared to be.

It wasn't that NAIC was a fly-by-night operation. It's just that it was totally dependent on people who donated their time and resources. If the economy took a hit, that support would quickly wane and with it, NAIC's ability to pay O'Hara.

There was no doubt that the organization was at a crossroads. It was growing so fast and there were so many economic developments and organizational challenges and opportunities that needed to be addressed every day that the Trustees were more than ready for Tom O'Hara when he asked the Board to make him a permanent and fulltime employee, charged with guiding and directing the work.

For a few weeks, as he transitioned out of the accountant's job, he ran back and forth across town between the School Board and the NAIC offices. But by spring, he had just one job: NAIC Chairman and Executive Director.

It didn't take long for him to wonder if he had made a terrible mistake.

NAIC Treasurer Bob Burger stopped by the office one day in May bearing some bad news.

After a couple of months of paying O'Hara a salary roughly equal to what he earned at the School Board, NAIC was almost out of money.

How could this be? O'Hara was flabbergasted. Before taking the job he and Eleanor, and even the Board of Trustees, had carefully examined the books. Counting current membership and projected growth they were convinced that the payroll of one could be met.

What went wrong?

Burger had an answer. He pulled out his ledger sheets. His review of the books showed that twelve hundred of the organization's roughly 2,800 member clubs lagged a year behind in their dues. That meant the sparse budget was considerably less rosy than they had anticipated.

There were two choices: Either O'Hara would have to figure out a way to get the delinquent dues into the NAIC bank account fast, or he would soon have to lay himself off.

O'Hara opted for the former.

Working almost around the clock for two days, using Eleanor, Burger and every other NAIC board member he could press into emergency service, O'Hara managed to get twelve hundred invoices written, stuffed into stamped envelopes and driven to the post office.

In the weeks following, several hundred clubs ignored those

invoices and NAIC withdrew their membership. But several hundred of them did pay their back dues. Some even paid for a year in advance. And dozens of new clubs joined and sent in their fees.

Money came in. O'Hara saved his job.

But then a potentially much more serious problem surfaced.

From time to time over the past couple of years, NAIC Board members had fielded polite inquiries from security regulatory agencies in various states. It was all new to them, the concept of small groups of individual investors banding together in clubs and buying small but regular amounts of stock. There were questions that the Trustees routinely answered, about how stock was bought through brokers, who held the stock certificates and how the clubs handled bookkeeping. No one at NAIC thought there were any concerns.

But apparently there were.

Indeed, as O'Hara learned, NAIC's growing club membership was being eyed with proprietary concern by securities regulators. In Ohio, legislation had been submitted that would require investment clubs to register each year with the state's Securities Commission and pay a registration fee. The last thing NAIC club members wanted was a new set of paperwork and additional fees. O'Hara and other board members were convinced that if Ohio enacted such a rule, other states would follow and the result would be a chilling effect on the formation of new clubs.

O'Hara wasn't concerned about the U.S. Securities and Exchange Commission. NAIC had done its homework long before and had been assured by federal regulators that as long as twenty-five or fewer people were involved in an investment club, the SEC would not be interested in imposing new regulations or forms.

Nobody thought to check with the individual state regulatory agencies. O'Hara and the other Trustees assumed that the SEC's hands-off policy would apply to NAIC clubs by states as well. The prospect of dozens of state security commissions requiring NAIC clubs to fill out forms and pay fees each year was a bureaucratic nightmare.

But that is precisely what the situation in Ohio threatened to unleash.

Something had to be done. If Ohio started regulating investment clubs, it would certainly be copied in state after state.

O'Hara pulled out the NAIC club membership roster and began working the phones. He mobilized club members across the state. In Columbus, one of the NAIC investment clubs boasted a member of the Ohio legislature, who, like other club members across the Buckeye State, was strongly opposed to the proposed regulation. Tom O'Hara set up a series of strategy meetings. Every Tuesday morning he got up at four in the morning and drove from Detroit to the Ohio capital of Columbus, a five hour trip. He spent the day meeting other legislators, explaining NAIC's grass roots operations and why a registration fee would pose an undue burden on clubs. He also met with influential members of the Ohio business community and asked them to plead the NAIC case with legislators and politicians.

Gradually, Tom O'Hara picked up another skill, that of a lobbyist. It was not a job he particularly liked and it took a toll. He developed severe migraines.

They affected him on just one day of the week, Tuesday.

Like clockwork, they hit when he slid behind the wheel of his car in the pre-dawn darkness. They began with a tightening in the back of his neck. As he drove down into Ohio it would gradually spread upwards and across. Eventually his forehead pounded as if in a vise.

For three months, he never said a thing to anyone about the migraines. He worked through them.

Then came the good news. The lobbying efforts had paid off. The Ohio Securities Commission decided to table the proposed rule additions. NAIC clubs did not have to register in the State of Ohio.

O'Hara's migraines stopped and never returned.

But the reprieve was brief.

A few weeks after Ohio abandoned its regulatory plans for investment clubs, a call came in from some NAIC friends at the New York Stock Exchange. They had word that the North American Securities Administration (The Association of State Security Commissions) had appointed a committee to study investment clubs and recommend whether or not all states should pass legislation regulating them.

This was even worse than Ohio's plan, which, if enacted would have at least taken a while to make its way across the country. If the

North American Securities Administration really required clubs to file papers and pay fees it would take immediate effect in every state.

The Committee, O'Hara learned, was composed of the Securities Commissioners of Wisconsin, Ohio and Michigan. O'Hara knew the Ohio chairman from his lobbying efforts there. He wondered if the national move was motivated because of the Ohio chairman's rebuff. O'Hara didn't think he could count on support from the Ohio commissioner.

The Michigan representative was Jack Hueni. George Nicholson knew him and thought he was a reasonable man. At best, O'Hara figured, it was one and one. The tie breaker would be the Chairman of the Committee, Ed Samp of Wisconsin. As O'Hara made calls and checked around, everyone described Samp as the driving force on the committee. If the idea was to be stopped, Samp was the stopper. He was the man O'Hara had to convince. If Samp could be convinced about the value of investment clubs and the need to make it as easy as possible for them to buy and sell their stocks, then, like Ohio, the North American Securities Administration would, hopefully, scuttle the plan.

Somehow, O'Hara needed to informally meet Samp and present the NAIC case to him. But how? Where? When? O'Hara determined that the three commissioners on the study committee had no formal meeting place or schedule.

Just as O'Hara was planning a trip to Madison, Wisconsin, a phone call from one of his friends at the New York Stock Exchange gave new urgency to the problem. The source informed O'Hara that the committee was supposed to meet and report to the full session of the administrators at their up-coming convention in Mexico City.

"If you're going to make your case, Tom," counseled the telephone tipster, "your only chance will be in Mexico City."

The caller added that it was probably a good idea for O'Hara to take his wife along, since most of the administrators brought their spouses. He was grateful his friend made the suggestion. Eleanor deserved a break. Besides, he had been gone so much since he took the full-time NAIC position that it was almost as if he still had two jobs. A trip to Mexico would perk her up. O'Hara delighted at the prospect of having his wife along.

Little did he know that she would be the key to making the trip a success.

O'Hara had a few weeks to prepare. George Nicholson set up a meeting with Jack Hueni, the Michigan Securities Commissioner. Hueni had glowing things to say about George Nicholson and said he had heard great things about NAIC and its efforts to educate investors. He volunteered to help O'Hara meet Samp at the convention.

O'Hara worked the phones again, using a network of NAIC members and friends across the country, hoping to find out why the national securities group was even thinking about requiring investment clubs to register. No one had an explanation. O'Hara reviewed trade publications and newspaper stories, but failed to turn up any clues. As best he could tell, no club had ever been victimized by securities fraud. Neither could he find any case anywhere in which an investment club had been involved in any kind of problem that could lead to state regulation. NAIC heard through the grapevine about a couple of cases where members of an individual club stole club assets, but these were minor incidents, involving insignificant funds and nothing of the sort that would cause security regulators to become concerned.

Even Jack Hueni wasn't sure why the committee he was on was looking into club regulation. "I think the commissioners are just being cautious," he told O'Hara.

Tom O'Hara would urge the committee members to forego any kind of investment club legislation. He knew he could explain how NAIC clubs operated, how every member took part in all the club decisions and how the NAIC structure minimized the potential for any type of securities fraud to develop. He would tell the committee that NAIC had a spotless track record. He'd say there just was no real reason for the states to regulate investment clubs.

But O'Hara did not like acting as a lobbyist. He remembered the migraines during the earlier Ohio crisis and prayed they wouldn't come back.

As he and Eleanor handed their tickets to the airline clerk at the Detroit airport on their way to the convention in Mexico, he realized, with considerable apprehension, that he still had no idea how to present NAIC's story to the Committee.

The first leg of the trip took the O'Hara's to Chicago. As they waited at the bustling O'Hare airport for the connecting flight to Mexico City, Tom opened his briefcase and buried himself in his work. Eleanor struck up a conversation with the woman sitting next to her. Soon, the woman's husband joined in. O'Hara was deep in thought about how he would meet the people he needed to meet when something about the voice of the man Eleanor was talking to caught his attention. He knew that voice.

It was Jack Hueni. The two had only talked on the phone. Now, thanks to Eleanor O'Hara, Tom O'Hara found himself shaking hands with one of the three men whose vote could determine the fate of NAIC.

The two couples hit it off right from the start. They laughed and joked and talked about kids until their flight was called. At one point on the five-hour flight, Hueni tried to reassure O'Hara about Ed Samp, the committee chairman. Samp, said Hueni, had a reputation as a gruff man, distant and sometimes stern.

"But he's honest and fair," said Hueni. "If you can get him to make time for you, he'll listen with an open mind."

They arrived in Mexico City, cleared customs, and piled into a taxi to make their way to the convention hotel downtown, a huge, sprawling complex that looked to O'Hara like the Capitol Building in Washington DC. A long series of steps led up from the street to the entrance and as the O'Hara's and their new friends started up Jack Hueni tugged at O'Hara's arm.

"Tom, you are in luck," said Hueni, gesturing to the top of the steps. "That's Ed Samp up there. Come on, I'll introduce you right now."

They hurried up the steps and Hueni and Samp exchanged greetings. Then he introduced O'Hara.

O'Hara didn't have time to think up a clever introduction. He shook the influential committee chairman's hand and just blurted it out.

"Ed, I have got something to talk about with you, could we sit together for dinner tonight?"

For a brief, silent moment, Samp stared at the young stranger. Then he looked at Hueni. Then back at O'Hara.

His voice was not rude. But it wasn't very friendly, either. Samp made it quite clear he had other plans for dinner. He then turned and walked into the lobby.

At lunch, O'Hara was convinced his career as a lobbyist had ended before it could really begin. Hueni tried to cheer up his new friend, taking him around the tables and introducing him to other State Security Commissioners.

"Here's a man you need to meet," he said, elbowing O'Hara to one of the up-front tables. "This is the Securities Commissioner for New York."

The man recognized Hueni and clasped his hand warmly. Hueni introduced O'Hara and the man smiled warmly. But as O'Hara reached across the table to shake hands, he bumped into a glass of ice water and knocked it directly into the lap of the commissioner.

The commissioner jumped up as conversation for several tables around halted and all eyes focused on the man with the napkin trying to blot out the spreading dark stain on the front of his expensive and well-tailored suit trousers. The man was good-natured about it, even managing a laugh. O'Hara was shell-shocked and red-faced and apologized profusely. But the man didn't seem upset. He just said, "Accidents happen," and he remained at the table until lunch was over.

O'Hara was more convinced than ever that his cause was lost.

Still, he spent the afternoon listening to several convention speakers, wondering how he could recover from his first impressions. Back in the room, he waited for Eleanor to return. She had gone off with Hueni's wife to see some of the sights and do some shopping. Late in the afternoon she returned. She beamed, the afternoon had been a great success. She said she had met a great bunch of ladies and one had been very friendly, and had invited the O'Haras to sit at her table that night.

The lady's name was Mrs. Samp.

O'Hara looked heavenward. It was as if it was divine providence. He was delighted he had brought his wife to the convention. But he wondered what Ed Samp would think when he sat down at his table that night.

Eleanor had accomplished by accident, what O'Hara hadn't been able to do. She just smiled and shrugged. "It will be a wonderful evening," she told her husband. "Just you wait and see."

She was right, too.

O'Hara had learned his lesson about the direct approach. At dinner, he was as charming as he could be. He and Samp talked several times during the meal but O'Hara kept it light and general, not mentioning a word about his mission.

The next morning, O'Hara and Samp passed each other in a hallway. This time, the Chairman recognized O'Hara and smiled a greeting. O'Hara made his move, this time to a friend. O'Hara explained NAIC's concern over the proposed regulation.

"Ed, would it be possible for me to speak to your committee at your meeting, to present our side of this issue?"

Samp seemed much less gruff than the previous day on the hotel stairway. He told O'Hara he needed to think about it. It was an unusual request. The committee was not taking testimony or hearing witnesses. "I'll get back to you," he said. But he said it with a warmth that gave O'Hara a lot more hope than he had the day before. Besides, there was time. It was only the first full day of a three-day convention and O'Hara read in the program that the investment club committee would not meet until the end of the third day.

Learning to be a lobbyist at that convention turned out to be a lot more fun than Tom O'Hara thought. Exhibitors, brokerage houses and various parts of the securities industry vied to entertain the regulators and convention-goers. At the meals held in the hotel, there were Flamenco dancers, mariachi singers and musicians, magicians and every kind of entertainment imaginable. Conventioneers were treated to a bull-fight and a motorcycle race. They went to an elaborate party at a private home built into the side of a mountain. A courtyard garden covered an area that looked as big as two city blocks back in Detroit. The dining room table was cut from a huge piece of stone that seemed to come right out of the mountain.

The delegates toured an oil refinery. They ate still more meals in elegant private clubs. They were bussed miles up into the mountains where huge metal tubes carried water down to electric turbines in the valley. One of the tubes was unused and the tourists rode down inside it on small railway cars to the turbines below.

On the third day, they were taken to a luxury golf resort located an hour's ride from the city on a triangular plateau high in the mountains. Meetings were scheduled throughout the day at various banquet rooms at the club. Whenever there was a pause in business a mariachi band serenaded the group. That night there would be a spectacular fireworks display, fired from the edge of the plateau overlooking the twinkling lights of Mexico City far below.

It was at the golf club event that O'Hara hoped to appear before Ed Samp's committee. On the trip to the resort he talked briefly with Samp. Samp's news threatened to spoil a perfectly wonderful day.

"Tom," said the chairman, "I've decided I can't permit you to attend the committee meeting. We just are not hearing from outsiders."

O'Hara's heart sank.

But Samp continued. "However, if you want to, you can write out your reasons why you think investment clubs should not be required to register with each state's security commission. If you do that, I will be pleased to present your paper to the committee."

O'Hara wished he had more time to prepare. But he knew his case. For two hours he wrote and rewrote. He handed his paper over to Samp just as the afternoon meeting began behind closed doors.

O'Hara never did get a full report on exactly what happened in the meeting or whether there was much debate. He knew Samp read his statement. Was impressed enough by it to include it word for word in the printed proceedings of the convention that was mailed out to their members in every state.

The proposed regulation was tabled for a year.

NAIC had some breathing room.

Over the next year, there were a couple of minor scares. The securities commissions in Tennessee and New Mexico did pass legislation on clubs. However, in both cases the law provided a size recommendation that exempted most NAIC clubs.

When the North American Association of Securities Regulators convened the next year, the committee's agenda permitted the appearance of anyone who wanted to comment on the proposed legislation. O'Hara was quick to take them up on the offer. He was the only outsider and he pretty much repeated, in person, the statement he had submitted the previous year. As they listened and then questioned him, it became apparent that none of the securities administrators were aware of any regulatory problems involving investment clubs. The Committee again recommended that no action be taken until the following year.

The third year it was tabled again.

The fourth year showed how O'Hara's effective lobbying efforts on behalf of NAIC had succeeded. Before O'Hara even requested his routine annual appearance before the Investment Club Committee at the Security Administrators Annual meeting, he received a call from Ed Samp.

This time, Samp wanted O'Hara to do more than express opposition to the plan. He wanted O'Hara to give the committee a full-blown report on the growth of the investment club movement. He did so with great delight, and when he finished Ed Samp thanked him profusely, with genuine warmth and respect and announced that the regulators were disbanding their committee on investment clubs.

It was a great day for NAIC and its members. Since then, a strong, solid professional relationship of trust and respect between NAIC and the state security regulators has continued and grown.

Over the years, a lot of people have tried to credit Tom O'Hara's lobbying efforts for averting the potentially disastrous regulation of investment clubs. But O'Hara just shrugs it off. He says he owes it all to Eleanor.

As it turned out, that Mexico City trip was just the start of the O'Hara's traveling for NAIC.

For the next several years, they spent weekends and summer vacations on the road, crisscrossing the country, evangelizing the NAIC investment principles to just about anyone who'd listen, just about anywhere. And it wasn't just Tom and Eleanor. The O'Hara boys went too. The family wore out two station wagons from the late fifties to the mid-sixties.

Besides the strong relationship with the regulatory agencies in individual states, things had certainly improved since Tom O'Hara's first frustrating trip to New York City and his visit to the New York Stock Exchange.

In 1955, Keith Funston, Chairman of the New York Stock Exchange, was the keynote speaker at the NAIC annual convention. He was most impressed by what he saw and, over the years, became a strong booster of the Association. The Exchange even printed its own folder on investment clubs and sent it out free of charge to the sales staffs at its member firms. One day in 1959, O'Hara got an idea. He called Funston in New York, and asked if Funston would be willing to arrange a series of meetings with securities salesmen. O'Hara would explain NAIC and suggest techniques the salesmen could employ to encourage the formation of investment clubs.

Funston liked the idea. As an experiment, the two agreed to five meetings in five different cities, lasting one week each month for five months.

They scheduled two meetings per day for a week. The first one didn't start until four-thirty or so in the afternoon, after the markets closed. All of the brokers for member firms in the city were invited to that meeting. O'Hara spent a half hour describing different ways brokers were working with investment clubs around the country, and how the brokers developed profitable radiation business handling personal investments for individual club members.

Then, after dinner, typically around seven thirty, the brokers would invite their customers to a meeting where O'Hara described the operation of investment clubs and how these clubs could be used as a classroom to help everyday people easily learn sound investment principles.

Sometimes, brokers joined O'Hara, serving as living examples. People like George Barnes of Thompson and McKinnon, and Tracey Freeman of Merrill Lynch, had been very successful at building their businesses with the help of clubs. Each were handling many dozens of clubs and had developed hundreds of individual customers.

At other times, though, O'Hara spoke alone. Instead of packed meeting rooms, he found himself making his NAIC pitch to only a handful of people.

That's because in some cities, the person the New York Stock Exchange had asked to set up the NAIC meeting was very protective of his territory. He didn't want to share information with competition, so only his salesmen and his customers got the NAIC information. Many times in those first couple of months O'Hara drove across the Midwest from Detroit to some new city like St. Louis or Cincinnati or Duluth. He unlimbered his lanky frame from the stiffness of being behind the wheel for so long. Then he worked up a sweat unloading boxes and files of NAIC literature from the back of the station wagon. He lugged it all into a hotel meeting room only to find, instead of a packed room, only four or five salesmen there.

It didn't take long to realize that he couldn't count on the local firm chosen by the Exchange to spread the word. So, once he selected a city, O'Hara sent notices to all the brokerage firms in the area.

Still, there were surprises. On one occasion O'Hara was disheartened when only two men showed up at the meeting. Hadn't his notices arrived, he asked the men? They had. It's just that in that town, they explained, there were only two brokerage firms. One of the firms had just hired all the employees of the competing firm. The two men who showed up to meet with O'Hara were the owners.

The disloyal employees weren't about to come back to the office they had just fled and face the wrath of their former bosses.

Undaunted, O'Hara proceeded to tell the audience of two all about NAIC. As it turned out, in the following months they went on to apply the tips they learned that night with great success.

The evening meetings that were open to the public also proved to be challenging. These, too, needed to be promoted and O'Hara sent out advance notices to newspapers and radio stations prior to each appearance. But the real success of the public sessions also depended on the local brokerage firms and how much effort they put into spreading the word. Sometimes the meetings were quite small. Others attracted several hundred people. At the evening meeting O'Hara gave a short talk on the history of NAIC, describing its investment philosophy and demonstrating how anyone could discern a company's investment potential by using NAIC's Stock Selection Guide. Across the country, people loved the idea that there was a simple but reliable way to predict how high and how low a stock might sell.

But there were also embarrassing glitches on the road.

There was usually not much information promoting a meeting, other than the address of an auditorium, building or hotel. One day O'Hara wound up in the headquarters auditorium of the "76" Union Oil company in San Francisco. That was all well and good. Except that as his example of a stock to study that night, O'Hara had prepared a chart on Standard Oil of Ohio. Three "76" executives were at the meeting and had a lot of fun watching his face turn red as he tried to save the program by frequently reminding his audience that surely the figures for "76" would look better on the Stock Selection Guide.

On another occasion, he wound up in the auditorium of Carrier Refrigeration and had a study of Trane Air Conditioning to present to the audience.

Still, as with the broker's meetings, the public sessions were very effective in building NAIC's membership. For a week or two after every series of meetings, applications from new clubs poured into the Detroit headquarters. It was not unusual to have as many as fifty new clubs join after a week on the road.

At the end of the six-month experiment, the NAIC board voted unanimously to continue the trips. Nobody could think of a more effective way of building membership than to turn Tom O'Hara loose on the country.

For several years, Tom O'Hara was a traveling salesman for NAIC. The trips were an O'Hara family affair. Eleanor helped drive and served as a greeter at the evening meetings. The boys came, too, and made a grand game out of every mile, counting license plates from different states and different car colors, coloring in the back seat, singing songs, learning about the country.

When the boys were young, the trips lasted as long as two weeks.

Each trip would begin with a prayer for safety. Eleanor strictly enforced this. And after traveling to every end of the continental United States for almost four years, after 200,000 miles under every imaginable type of weather, the prayers were always answered. They never experienced a simple accident or serious mechanical breakdown that couldn't be repaired in a few hours.

They divided the country into regional quarters and worked a whole section before heading back home. They drove straight through to their furthest destination, in the days before freeways, traveling mostly two lane state highways and, sometimes, unpaved, county roads. Five days to California and the West, six to the Pacific Northwest. Three days to Florida and the South, two to Boston and the East Coast. They held meetings in four or five good-sized cities over a week, and then headed back home, trying to squeeze in two or three more.

They crossed the Mojave Desert by car in the days before air conditioning. They carried extra water along and had to strap ice bags on the hood of the car.

They drove through Rocky Mountain rainstorms, blizzards on the Great Plains, freezing rain in Appalachia.

One time they were delayed by bad weather and road conditions coming into Sacramento and clearly wouldn't have time to find a motel. They drove straight to the meeting. Eleanor slid behind the wheel and sent Tom to the back seat where he changed into a clean white shirt and tie in front of the boys, who laughed hysterically.

But they never missed a scheduled meeting. Never.

Every person who attended a meeting received a copy of NAIC's magazine and the folder "An Educational and Investment Opportunity For You" that explained how to invest long term. Boxes of NAIC club manuals, accounting material and Stock Study Forms filled the O'Hara station wagon. Eleanor unloaded it every day, setting the material up for sale on a folding table at the back of the meeting room. The O'Hara's counted the week a great success when Eleanor sold enough to cover the trip's expenses.

As the boys grew older and started school, the family could only take the longer trips around school holidays, at Christmas and Easter. During the summer months, they traveled for two and three weeks at a time, speaking to as many as three thousand people in a dozen cities.

Along the way, the O'Haras made great friends. People invited them home for dinner. Packed them fried chicken picnic baskets. Sent them Christmas cards for decades.

Shelly, the O'Hara's daughter, missed all of those meetings because she didn't come along until 1964. By that time with shifts in the securities industry, and less interest in the individual investor, it became difficult to get brokers to sponsor those meetings. But Shelly made many trips with her father and mother to many Chapter meetings, especially the Northwest Ohio Chapter Spring Training sessions where representatives of a dozen or more Chapters enjoyed a weekend of forward planning and exchanging experiences. She became about as well known as her brothers.

The securities industry was booming. The economy was hot. Employment was high and public confidence in the stock market returned in a big way. Funston and the New York Stock Exchange, echoing the message from NAIC, had launched a massive "Own Your Share of America" campaign and the number of individual American shareholders grew from around six million to more than twenty million.

But with big growth came yet another problem.

Business reached such volume that some brokerage firms were simply unable to handle the demand. So many orders were coming in that many companies quit answering the phones and closed their entire sales operations several hours a day to process the paperwork. Even then, many couldn't keep up. As a result, there was a consolidation that swept through the industry. The big, regional and national brokerage houses eagerly sought out small family run operations and gobbled many of them up.

As the brokerage business got bigger, interest in the little guy, the small investor, started to diminish. It became increasingly difficult for O'Hara and NAIC to find brokers willing to set up informational meetings about forming investment clubs.

Slowly, in the early sixties, the road trips came to an end. A new dilemma took center stage requiring O'Hara's undivided attention back at NAIC headquarters.

Paperwork.

It all revolved around the sticky issue of stock certificates and who possessed them. In the early days, NAIC discovered four ways club securities could be held. The way that many clubs started in the early days was for stock of one company to be registered jointly in the names of two members. The second stock the club bought would be registered jointly in the names of two more members, and on down the line. The club received actual certificates for the securities and the treasurer kept them, physically, in a safe deposit box. It was cumbersome and took a lot of bookkeeping, but it worked.

A second and much improved way was for the club to form a legal partnership and for securities to be registered in the legal name of the club. Again, this meant that the club physically possessed the stock certificates, which involved a lot of mailing back and forth between the brokers and the club.

Brokers clearly didn't like either of the first two methods. Many were taking on club business only in hopes that they'd develop lucrative personal accounts for individual members. So working with a broker, they came up with a third way to transfer stock that allowed the securities to be held by the broker, on behalf of the club. In this way the broker had certificates issued to the club, but held them in his own vault.

A fourth, and even more simple procedure, was also tried by many brokers where stock would be issued directly to the broker in "street name," and held by him, although the stock was, of course, legally owned by the club.

But even with the evolution of the stock transfer procedures, a lot of brokerage firms grumbled. Many loudly complained that investment clubs were not worth the effort. Club accounts were generally small and did not generate much in the way of commissions. They did, however, generate considerable paperwork. That took time for the broker and, as they said, time is money.

Club members, however, didn't like the procedures that much either.

Many were distrustful that their certificates of ownership were in their broker's vaults. They preferred to hold their securities in their own hands, even though that involved extra work. The happenings associated with the 1929 crash were still on people's minds. People didn't trust brokers to hold their securities. Tensions were sometimes strong.

Then the issue arose about investment clubs that had organized themselves as legal partnerships. While it was relatively easy for a club to get a certificate issued, getting it out of its name when a club broke up or membership changed was another huge headache.

That involved yet a third player. Transfer agents, the people hired by public companies as "caretakers" for their shareholders. Transfer agents kept shareholder records and issued new certificates. They distributed proxies, dividends and annual reports, and they forwarded company correspondence to shareholders. They were extremely significant players in the investment process and they made life difficult for many clubs. They wanted still more paperwork, especially for partnerships. All too often, they required a maze of red tape. When a club sold a stock and presented the certificate to its broker, he sent it along to the stock transfer agent at the company. Then, more often than not, the transfer agent demanded a pile of papers. At the least, he wanted a statement proving that the club had passed a resolution authorizing the sale and at what price. Then, the agent often asked for a copy of a resolution passed by the club giving one partner the authority to make that transaction and sign the necessary documents. In most cases, every member was required to sign the certificate or a power of attorney before the shares could be transferred to someone else.

Caught between the grumbling brokers and the bureaucratic stock transfer agents, investment club treasurers started getting ulcers.

It was clear to Tom O'Hara that if the club movement was going to keep growing and serving the average small investor, something had to be done to streamline the process of club buying and selling.

With NAIC attorney Lew Rockwell, O'Hara started by networking with club members who worked for General Motors and American Telephone & Telegraph to make an introduction for them at their New York office. Influential club members arranged appointments with officials from these giant corporations and they in turn set up meetings with their stock transfer agents in New York. O'Hara and Rockwell flew to New York to discuss the situation with NAIC friends at the New York and American Stock Exchanges. The visits to the exchanges were pleasant, but the pair soon learned the exchanges were not at all involved in stock transfer or registry problems. They suggested NAIC contact Francis Christy, an officer and attorney for the Security Transfer Association, known as the "czar" of the stock transfer business.

At General Motors, O'Hara and Rockwell were greeted by a large contingency of the corporation's legal staff. An entire roomful of conservatively dressed attorneys filled a conference room in GM's Manhattan skyscraper. They assured the NAIC delegation of two that GM had no problem transferring securities in and out of a partnership's name on the signature of only one partner. However, the GM experts also suggested NAIC contact the same Francis Christy, himself an attorney and the key player in the Security Transfer Association. In their opinion the best solution to the paperwork problem would be for the association of stock transfer agents to pass a specific rule making it easy for investment club partnerships to buy and sell their stocks.

The next meeting, with investor relation's people at AT&T, confirmed that Christy was the person O'Hara and Rockwell must convince. To help, one of the AT&T representatives picked up the phone, called Christy's office, and arranged an appointment for the two first thing the next morning.

The Security Transfer Association held a tremendous amount of clout, not just on Wall Street and in New York City but in corporate boardrooms and financial centers across the country. Formed in 1911 as a trade association for "securities transfer processors," it consisted of influential corporate, bank and independent transfer agents, the people who perform the critical record keeping functions for publicly traded companies. Christy was the Association's point man. He authored textbooks on stock transfer, said the AT&T people. He was a sharp-minded, no-nonsense lawyer who personally directed much of the day-to-day transfer procedures that dictated the way investments were bought and sold.

"He's the guy that can make it easy for you. Or very difficult," one of the AT&T contacts told the NAIC men from Detroit. "It's all in his hands."

O'Hara said a few extra prayers that night.

Tom O'Hara and Lew Rockwell arrived at Christy's midtown law office a few minutes before the nine-thirty meeting. Christy wasn't there, said the receptionist with a smile. She was sure he'd arrive any minute, she explained, showing the Detroit visitors to a seat.

Time passed. Slowly. From time to time the embarrassed receptionist apologized, saying that Christy was usually very prompt, but for some reason, she had not heard anything from him.

For over an hour O'Hara and Rockwell waited. Just as they began to think they had been stood up, a very frustrated man barged through the door. It was Christy and he did not look happy.

"I'll be right with you," he said, moving directly into his office.

A couple of minutes later the receptionish ushered O'Hara and Rockwell in. From behind his desk, Christy explained that he had been caught in a traffic jam. He seemed a bit embarrassed'to be late, as if that sort of thing never should happen to a stock transfer agent. But he was also a man who clearly didn't indulge in small talk.

He cleared his throat and got right down to business. "What can I do for you?" he asked.

O'Hara told him about NAIC and its goal to educate everyday Americans about long-term investing, and how investment clubs were catching on rapidly. Rockwell explained how clubs were organized mostly as partnerships but that transfer agents were hesitant to transfer stock out of club names without a great many signatures and supporting papers.

Christy listened intently to both men.

When they finished, he was silent for a moment.

"I see," he said, "we're being a little stuffy and a little self-protective are we?"

O'Hara didn't want the man to think NAIC was insulting him. But before he could mutter words to placate him, Christy interrupted with a wave of his hand.

"Let me think about this for a minute," he said.

And he did. Christy sat still in his chair for a minute or two and then wrote a few words on a scratch pad and handed it to O'Hara. O'Hara grinned and handed it to Rockwell. He also grinned.

"How does that sound?" asked Christy.

It read: "Stock held by ABC Investment Club, a partnership, may be transferred on the signature of one partner. No supporting papers are required."

That was the simplest and most direct answer to the problem O'Hara and Rockwell could possibly think of, and they told Christy so without hesitation.

"Very well then," said the transfer agent "czar." The three men shook hands.

With a few minor additions, that quickly scribbled note eventually became the official rule, Number 13.06, of the Security Transfer Association.

NAIC had cleared yet another obstacle.

Tom O'Hara and Lew Rockwell's New York trip extinguished the external paperwork problems. However, back at NAIC headquarters, the organization itself was bogging down in its own internal difficulties.

It was the growing pains of success. The organization had grown so fast that it needed strong administrative control or would soon be bogged down by inefficiency.

Tom O'Hara needed some help.

NAIC was primarily a volunteer group. While Rockwell and others, inspired and prodded by George Nicholson, stood ready to help, they all worked at their own jobs. NAIC work was reduced to after hours and weekends. O'Hara persevered in non-stop days, his ears glued to the phone, his desk littered with telephone messages and letters from clubs and corporations. He attended frequent luncheon meetings, board meetings, and out of town business trips with not nearly enough time in the day to do all that needed to be done.

O'Hara hired several women to help with clerical duties. In the back mail room, a dozen part time college students helped in the afternoon, opening and sorting mail, gathering and sending out the literature requested by so many people in so many places.

By late summer, in 1960, O'Hara went to the NAIC board and got authorization for another full-time employee — an office manager and administrator.

He hired a pro.

A golf pro.

Chapter Five: The Making of "Mr. NAIC"

O ver the years, Ken Janke has become known as "Mr. NAIC." His solid, well-researched investment advice, coupled with his unswerving devotion to the NAIC principles of long-term investing, has been followed by tens of thousands of investors who have heard him in seminars across the country or read his monthly column in NAIC's *Better Investing* magazine. A lot of them have become wealthy because of Ken Janke.

"He knows his stuff," is what you often hear whispered in the back rows of folding chairs when Janke starts teaching one of his sessions at an NAIC meeting.

"He's got a knack for explaining this," others will say.

"Now I understand."

Janke's effective teaching tactics are legendary in NAIC circles.

But what most people don't know is that they were honed, not on the trading floor of a stock exchange or brokerage house, but on a golf course.

Ken Janke was a professional golfer.

And not just any golf pro. He was a U.S. Army golf pro who had, as he was quick to explain, perhaps the best job ever devised by the military.

Janke, an economics major who played golf on the Michigan State University Varsity team, was the Golf Professional at the beautifully-manicured Orleans Golf Club in Orleans, France.

He landed his golf career based on some advice he got from a fellow inductee when he joined the service in 1955. "Don't put down 'student' when they ask for your occupation," whispered a friend at the Army induction center. "Otherwise, you'll end up in the infantry."

So Janke just put down one word: "Golf."

It worked. Janke reported for duty on New Year's Day, 1956. In Basic Training, someone noticed that one word. Next thing Janke knew, he was the Assistant Pro at the Fort Dix Golf Club in New Jersey. For a year or so, Janke instructed the officers at Fort Dix and the nearby McGuire Air Force Base. Then, because of Cold War tensions with Russia and the communist bloc, Janke, and just about everyone in his graduating class, was shipped overseas. Assigned to Frankfurt, Germany, he was quickly summoned to meet with a Major.

The Major had Janke's file. Down in Orleans, France, the Major explained, an important base coordinated military communications for much of Europe. High morale was a priority for the personnel stationed there. Therefore, Uncle Sam had built them a brand new golf course. They needed a golf pro. Would Janke be interested?

That's how Ken Janke spent most of his military duty, teaching American Army officers how to play golf in the middle of the Cold War on a beautiful new course about an hour's drive from Paris. And what a life it was. The Army assigned him an apprentice valet to take care of all his personal and houshold needs. He lived in an eight-room house, the former servant quarters of an old chateau. A French maintenance crew manicured the greens. His staff included a cook, a bartender and a clerk.

A twenty-two year old, he pinched himself a lot.

Everything was perfect. Except for one thing. He missed a young woman named Sally.

They had met back at Dearborn High School, near Detroit, when Janke's family moved to the area from northern Ontario, Canada. They started dating in their junior year and then Janke won a golf scholarship to Michigan State. Sally enrolled there too, even though it greatly upset her brothers, who expected her to follow them to the University of Michigan, State's arch-rival.

They were inseparable for six years, two years of high school and four of college. Then came the Army. In 1956, half a world away, Janke, as perfect as his Army golf pro life was there in Orleans, pined for Sally.

She also missed him and one day announced, quite boldly, that she was going to France to get married. Right then and there.

They did, on a beautiful June day in 1957.

Janke served the rest of his military career in France and, when discharged from the service in 1958, returned with Sally to Detroit. It was good to get back to family. Even though Janke loved golf, he was anxious to relegate the links to his leisure time and start a new job that applied the economic skills he had developed in college. With a new job in the Detroit office of Household Finance, he soon settled into civilian life.

As part of his military discharge, Janke was required to join the Army reserves. It was there that he met Bob Burger.

Burger was Janke's commanding officer of the reserve battalion. He took a fast liking to his new enlisted man. Burger, the owner of K.C. Jones Plating Company in Detroit, moved up within the reserve command structure to become, by 1960, the Division Commander, he promoted Janke, too. Janke became the Sergeant Major.

The Janke's, who soon welcomed two small children, a son in 1958 and a daughter in 1959, were delighted with their lives. They lived in Dearborn, not far from their childhood homes. Grandparents lived nearby and watched their two small children. Janke actually enjoyed his Army reserve work. His job at Household was promising, too.

One day in the summer of 1960, Janke was called into the office of his boss at Household. It was a classic good news, bad news meeting.

The good news was that Household liked Ken Janke. The corporation liked him a lot. He was an up-and-coming manager and had a bright future ahead of him.

In Texas.

Texas? Janke was puzzled.

The manager explained that the State of Texas had just passed new legislation effective in January 1961, that would allow consumer finance companies to open loan offices throughout the state. Household Finance was planning a large presence in Texas and needed to transfer a lot of managers including Janke.

Janke did his best to smile. He knew refusing a transfer with a corporation like Household would be the equivalent of professional suicide.

Sally took the news with great disappointment. They had bought their house just six months before. It wasn't much, a small bungalow, but a huge step up from the upper flat they had rented since the discharge from the service. They were homeowners.

"Isn't there anything that could be done?" Sally asked.

Janke shook his head. In the corporate world in 1960, managers were chattel. Possessions. The company owned a man. When they said go, you went. He didn't see any alternatives.

But his reserve officer Bob Burger did.

"Let me ask you something, Ken," Burger asked the day Janke told him of the impending transfer to Texas. "Would you be interested in staying here in Michigan?"

Janke told him that Michigan was home and he and Sally and the kids didn't want to move.

"What would you say if I knew of a way you could stay here, earn more money than you are getting at Household and have a bright career that helps people far beyond anything you've ever experienced with that finance company?"

Janke knew that Burger did not exaggerate. His commanding officer had something definite in mind.

"What do I have to do?" he asked.

"Go meet my friend Tom O'Hara."

Janke knew that his commanding officer was a successful Detroit-area businessman with strong ties to the automobile industry. But what he didn't know was that Burger was also an original member of the Mutual Investment Club, a Board Member and Treasurer of NAIC, and a college fraternity brother of Tom O'Hara.

And Burger had been talking to O'Hara about Ken Janke.

The need for an NAIC Office Manager was obvious to the Board. It was time to give Tom O'Hara the help he needed. And Burger, who had watched and trained Ken Janke for two years while in the Reserves couldn't think of a better man. Janke had a keen managerial eye. Scrupulously honest, dedicated to detail, a family man, a pleasant conversationalist and financially savvy, he was a perfect fit for NAIC.

Besides, he was a scratch golfer.

The meeting was arranged late on a mid-September afternoon at the NAIC office in downtown Detroit's First National Building. Janke rushed over as soon as his Household office closed for the day. He did not want his boss to know about the interview for a new job. As the elevator rose to the twelfth floor, he realized that, whatever salary they offered him, if they offered him a job, he'd have to pay for parking. And that could run another $30-35 a week.

Janke liked Tom O'Hara even before he shook his hand. O'Hara's warm blue eyes and low-key friendliness immediately put him at ease. O'Hara told Janke all about NAIC, how he got involved right after college, how he knew Burger, the success the group had achieved, the satisfaction that came from helping thousands of people realize financial independence. Janke hung on every word. There was a sense of mission about all this. He saw it in O'Hara and he wanted it, too.

He did not have that same sense of mission at the finance company. Household was just a job. A corporate job. He had started as a trainee and then became assistant manager and finally branch manager. He did it all by just putting in the time and following the corporate instruction manual. Janke remembered a friend who had been promoted to a supervisory job at Household. When they promoted him, the friend later told O'Hara, they asked him if he knew why he was being promoted.

"Because I did a good job?" ventured the friend.

"No. You're being promoted because you followed the instruction manual."

Following a manual in Texas was not how Janke wanted to live out the rest of his working life.

There was no room for creativity in the structured corporate setting Household expected him to follow. As Janke watched and listened to Tom O'Hara explain NAIC, he realized that he wanted what Tom O'Hara had. Passion. Excitement. A belief in what he was doing. A sense of fulfillment. The knowledge that he was making a positive difference in the lives of people and thus, helping to strengthen the social and economic foundation of the nation itself.

This, Janke thought, as O'Hara's words sunk in, was a noble undertaking. A movement that he could give himself to wholeheartedly, creating not just a career but a legacy.

O'Hara took Janke on a tour of NAIC headquarters. Normally several women — secretaries and clerical workers filled the office, O'Hara explained, but they had gone home at five o'clock. O'Hara guided him to the mail room.

There, O'Hara explained, about ten young men, all college students and all part-timers, worked on average, fifteen to twenty hours a week. Everywhere white sacks marked "U.S. Mail" were overflowing with letters. Cardboard boxes for NAIC materials stood on tables and the men filled them and taped them shut. From a radio across the room the distinctive Southern twang of Ernie Harwell was called the action of a Detroit Tigers baseball game as the mail room workers went about their tasks.

Janke wasn't sure, but he had the impression that the pace of the activity increased as O'Hara stepped into the room.

"This is the nerve center for NAIC," explained O'Hara. "This is where the mail comes in, where it's sorted and processed and where we send out materials. Everything we do revolves around this room."

Janke just looked and nodded.

The two chatted a few more minutes and shook hands. O'Hara promised to get back to Janke later in the week.

Later turned out to be the next day. O'Hara called Janke at home and got right to the point. Bob Burger had recommended Ken Janke. That alone carried a tremendous amount of weight. And after meeting Janke, Tom O'Hara saw why Burger was so impressed. There was no need to interview anyone else. O'Hara offered Janke a salary greater than his Household income. Enough extra to pay the costs of parking, and eating lunch in downtown restaurants, Janke noted.

Janke wanted to accept right then and there. But he talked to Sally first. She was thrilled that they would be able to stay in Detroit.

He called O'Hara the next day and accepted, agreeing to start on October 1, 1960. But he had a condition, Janke said.

"I don't want you to tell them that I am the Office Manager," he told O'Hara. "I just want to work as one of them, back in the mail room, for a while. I want to learn how the letters come in, how mail is handled, the whole procedure. And it will be best if the boys think I'm just another worker. That way I'll understand the operation as it really is."

If O'Hara was surprised at the request, he didn't say a thing. He agreed.

On the first day, Janke showed up and went straight to the mail room. Nobody suspected a thing. He started out opening the mail and sorting it into piles. Requests for club membership information. Requests for literature and club bulletins. Dues payments. He moved on to stuffing envelopes. Grabbing documents. Folding them. Putting the envelopes in piles by city and state. Then he ran the little tin stamping machine that printed out addresses.

At the time, NAIC was in the middle of a promotional mailing for Value Line, the investment research company whose painstakingly detailed financial surveys and reports had long been a key means by which NAIC members obtained the investment information needed to complete their Stock Selection Guide research on various companies. Sending targeted mailings to club members accounted for a part of NAIC's revenues. Although it would have been easier for the

Association to simply turn over its membership lists to companies, NAIC determined early on to carefully guard those names and not to give them to anyone else. So, while companies were free to send promotions to NAIC members, the actual mailing was controlled by NAIC and the companies were never given a complete list. Instead, they "rented" the list by sending the promotional materials to NAIC, whose own personnel then stuffed the letters and mailed them out.

The job was all done by hand. It didn't take Janke long to see the need for some major efficiencies. Work was leisurely at best with lots of joking and laughing. A lot of letters were misplaced by careless workers, and had to be resorted. People came to work late and left early.

About two o'clock in the afternoon on his second day on the job, the undercover manager posing as the mail boy walked past a far corner of the mail room and noticed one of the workers sound asleep, sprawled across a stack of mail bags from the Post Office.

Janke couldn't help himself.

He shook the guy awake. "Hey, what's the matter with you? Aren't you supposed to be working?"

The worker scrambled to his feet, red-faced, and returned to his job.

Janke worked in the mail room for two weeks. Towards the end, he figured the other workers knew he wasn't one of them. For one thing, while pleasant, he did his job. Though brand new to the work, he stuffed and opened more envelopes in one hour than the others did in two or three. It didn't help that, several times a day, Tom O'Hara would come back and quietly confer with Janke, sometimes even suggesting that he join him for a cup of coffee.

After two weeks, Janke had seen enough, both in the mail room and in the front office, where four women worked as secretaries. It seemed like every time he passed by the women they were taking a coffee break. Or visiting with each other.

"Okay, Tom, I need to know what my responsibility is here and how much authority I have," said Janke one day to O'Hara.

"You are the manager," said O'Hara. "You can do pretty much as you want to. These people work under you and you are responsible for this office running at maximum efficiency."

Janke wanted to be absolutely sure. "I can hire and fire?"

"That is your responsibility," confirmed O'Hara.

"Based on what I have observed over these past two weeks, then," said Janke, "there are some changes I think should be made in the personnel."

"Go right ahead," said O'Hara.

Janke cleaned house.

In the mail room, he fired five of the ten workers, including the one he caught sleeping on the sacks of mail.

The five part-timers who kept their jobs suddenly accomplished more than when there were ten.

Out in the main office, he fired three of the four secretaries and clerical workers. He brought in two women he knew from Household Finance to replace the three that were fired.

The office hummed.

At last with Janke firmly in control of the NAIC office, Tom O'Hara could concentrate on what he did best — organizing, building and improving the organization. Janke took firm control of the office and headquarters' operations. The two quickly settled into a comfortable leadership routine, meeting several times a day to delegate the workload and brainstorm.

Janke's immediate concern, once the office staff worked efficiently, was income. NAIC was a volunteer organization. But to succeed, that organization required strong organizational support. And that took money. Club dues, paid timely, certainly helped. One of the first things Janke did was set up an effective record-keeping system so that renewal invoices were promptly sent out. He also made sure that only paid-up members received the NAIC magazine and that membership rolls were current and regularly culled of inactive and delinquent members.

But new revenue was also needed, he explained to O'Hara, to keep pace with the growing demands for more services. And that took him back to the mail room.

The mail room ran in spurts. After a magazine or newspaper ran a story about NAIC, letters and requests for information would pour in and the mail room workers were busy for days. However, there were often a couple of days each week when the workload sagged and the workers would have more time on their hands than Janke liked. The problem was, there was no way of accurately predicting the demand. So the mail room had to be fully staffed. The extra work and income that came from mailing out material from firms like Value Line certainly helped. It would be nice to get some more, Janke thought. But how?

Tom O'Hara gave him the idea. They were walking around the mail room one day and O'Hara pointed out that NAIC mailed out an annual report to all of its members each year on the performance of the companies whose stocks were most often bought by the member clubs.

"That's the kind of mailing our members seem to appreciate," said O'Hara in passing the file cabinet that contained the annual reports on club holdings. "They are really interested in performance information."

The light bulb went off.

Janke spent the next week or so in his office writing letters to drug companies. At the time, that's where the action was. New medicines were coming on the market nearly every day and the pharmaceutical market was booming. Janke acquired the Standard & Poor's report on the major drug companies and then wrote the corporate treasurers. He told them that they had quite a story to tell and offered for them to tell that story to tens of thousands of individual investors. He then informed them of the NAIC membership list and said that the NAIC headquarters would be willing to mail out the annual reports for the various companies.

Three drug companies took Janke up on his offer and hired NAIC to mail out their reports.

Then Janke had another idea.

His research revealed a booming pharmaceutical industry. It also identified the steel industry as foundering, hit hard by overseas competition. The steel industry clearly needed more shareholders. He wrote the leading steel producers and told them he knew how they could get in touch with a huge audience of potential investors.

Immediately, two companies, Inland Steel and U.S. Steel, contracted to send out their annual reports and investor literature to NAIC member clubs.

In weeks, the NAIC mail room was so busy that Janke hired workers and the association's income improved dramatically.

Six months after he hired Janke, Tom O'Hara sent a report to the Trustees saying, for the first time, NAIC was making a profit. Janke's efficiencies and marketing skills were paying off.

Janke read O'Hara's note with a strong sense of pride and accomplishment. As he was about to file it away he noticed a slip of paper clipped to it. "Since we're doing so well we should consider pay increases for everyone." It was signed Thomas C. O'Hara.

Puzzled, Janke went next door to his boss's office.

"What do you want me to do about the raises?" he asked.

O'Hara was also puzzled. "What raises?"

Janke handed over the note. O'Hara broke out in a huge grin.

"Somebody's putting you on," he laughed. "That's not my signature. They're trying to pull a fast one."

The two shared a good laugh at the ruse. Janke never did find out who wrote the note.

However, the next week he was pleasantly surprised to receive a pay raise for himself, a raise that Tom O'Hara personally authorized with his real signature.

Besides organizing the NAIC office, Janke also learned NAIC from the inside. Right after he came aboard, he organized an investment club with some of his friends and even some workers from the mail room. He made sure that he was the Treasurer of the Club so he could answer any of the accounting questions that came to headquarters from members. He diligently learned, and then mastered, the NAIC Stock Selection Guide form. His hands-on experience often came in handy during the workday when frustrated new members called headquarters with questions. Janke frequently dropped whatever he was doing and patiently talked them through the procedures.

Even his wife, Sally, joined an investment club. She took to it so well that she was soon teaching seminars.

Still, not everything was a success.

In the mid-sixties, when the market took a slight drop and membership slowed, O'Hara and Janke, spurred on by George Nicholson, hired an advertising agency. The agency convinced the

NAIC executives to take out a newspaper ad. Although the association had never done any advertising before it agreed to give it a try. The agency said that the most popular part of a newspaper was the comics section and that the Sunday comics section was the best place to be noticed.

The *Cleveland Post* was selected and the space ads purchased. It was a lot of money, but the agency convinced them that it would pay off.

Not a single request for information came in from the ads.

It was an expensive but valuable lesson.

There would be no more such advertising.

But public relations was a different matter. Almost all of the NAIC growth spurts could be traced back to newspaper or magazine coverage of NAIC and investment clubs.

Janke and O'Hara met with Nicholson. The three concluded that having third parties tell the NAIC story was more effective than trying to "sell" themselves through ads.

The advertising budget was shifted into PR. Janke and O'Hara wrote news releases about successful clubs. They offered O'Hara as an interview subject to financial publications looking for information and quotes about the market and the individual investor. They regularly pitched story ideas about the need for long-term investment and educated investors. One of the publications that saw the news value of NAIC was Readers Digest. Its story on the Association in the mid-sixties brought over twelve thousand letters from people all over the world seeking information on how to start investment clubs.

The response overwhelmed the NAIC office. More bags of mail arrived each day. Like O'Hara had done before, Janke, took stacks of mail home. He and Sally attacked the mail together, working late into the night after the kids had gone to sleep. Sally pecked away on a portable typewriter, addressing mailing stickers, which the office staff tore off and attached to envelopes the next day. Because they only had one typewriter, Janke used a pen to write others out by hand.

After a few weeks, the Readers Digest mail deluge ended and several thousand new investment club members joined the NAIC roster.

All this new activity and growth severely strained the office space. Every desk overflowed. Stacked boxes filled every corner. People bumped into each other. It was time to move.

During the mid-Sixties, Washington Boulevard in Detroit was like Fifth Avenue in New York. And one of the most prestigious addresses on that boulevard was the Washington Boulevard Building. It was prestigious because it actively sought out prestigious tenants. And NAIC, basking in the glow of favorable national publicity, was exactly the kind of tenant the Washington Boulevard Building wanted to attract. Janke and O'Hara negotiated an incredible lease. If NAIC agreed to sign a three-year agreement, the building owners would absorb all the costs of the move. They offered the Association space nearly twice the size of the First National Building offices, with the cost less than what NAIC was currently paying.

The move to the larger office added to the professionalism of the Association. So did new printing machines. The old blue mimeograph used to print much of NAIC's literature was replaced by a new, more efficient, high-speed multigraph machine that printed crisp, clean black type. A second machine was bought and used to print letterhead stationary. In-house production saved even more money.

O'Hara, meanwhile, still traveled all across the country. At least once a month, he drove to meet with investment brokers during the day and the public at night.

He started taking Ken Janke with him. At first, Janke simply observed O'Hara as he addressed the audience, standing in the back of the room, manning the NAIC table and selling Association bulletins and publications. At the end of the day, O'Hara sat down with Janke and discussed the lessons of the day. After several trips, O'Hara assigned Janke specific portions of the talk. Then at dinner, O'Hara critiqued Janke's performance. The sections he covered would change regularly until, eventually, Janke knew the entire NAIC presentation.

The association kept growing.

The three-year lease on Washington Boulevard passed quickly. And that posed a major dilemma. By 1969, NAIC was again bursting at the seams even in the new building.

For some time, Tom O'Hara had been investigating the possibility of buying a building, instead of leasing office space. Hard times hit Detroit. In 1967 there had been terrible race riots that, almost overnight, caused scores of businesses to shut down and move to the suburbs. Perhaps it was unwise to lease in a decaying central city.

The first place O'Hara showed Janke was a real bargain, a funeral home in Pontiac, some thirty-five miles north of Detroit. It could be easily converted into an office building, but none of the board members liked the idea of an organization devoted to vitality and growth located in a former funeral home. They quickly scrapped the idea. They also considered an industrial building in midtown Detroit at the intersection of two freeways. The costs involved in remodeling it to accommodate NAIC were excessive. Finally, after seeking the service of a commercial real estate broker, they found the perfect building.

It was on Eleven Mile Road in Royal Oak, three miles north of the Detroit city limits and not far from O'Hara's and Janke's homes. It was a former S&H Green Stamps redemption center. It was perfect, except for an all-glass front, which they easily replaced with brick walls. The basement housed the mail room and print shop. Offices and conference rooms occupied the main street level. They completed the move in 1970.

Janke and O'Hara grew closer throughout this time period. For O'Hara, an only child, Janke was like a kid brother. To Janke, O'Hara was like a big brother. Their two families became close friends, too, often vacationing together.

O'Hara's friends became Janke's friends.

It was only natural that Janke would be invited to join O'Hara at his frequent lunches with George Nicholson.

Each luncheon meeting followed a pattern.

It started with O'Hara explaining to Nicholson some current NAIC challenge or opportunity. Nicholson quickly made his observations and suggestions and then launched into an involved discussion about politics and the economy or some specific investment subject.

Janke seldom said a thing. He listened to Nicholson and marveled at the depth of the man's knowledge. Janke's head often swam with facts, figures and theories. Nicholson passionately believed that it was the collective power of individual investors that made the U.S. the most stable nation in the world. He was always teaching, always seeing new trends in financial reports and government statistics and he poured out his wisdom in a flood of words that, at times, overwhelmed his eager mealtime student.

But finally, on the way back to the office one afternoon after a couple of years of these weekly Nicholson luncheons, Janke told O'Hara, only half facetiously, "Wow, I think I almost understand what George said."

O'Hara laughed. "It took me about two years to understand what George was saying, too."

While O'Hara and Janke had been building the investment club movement nationally, George Nicholson had been busy globally.

Having proven that his idea to mass produce educated and successful individual investors through investment clubs worked domestically, Nicholson envisioned that they could be used across the world to accomplish the same thing in every country. He passionately believed a financially educated, financially stable populace was the best defense against totalitarianism and communism. Individual investors shored up individual businesses and served as a natural check and balance against bad government. He told anyone who would listen.

A lot of people did listen. The publicity about the association and the many success stories told by investment clubs in the U.S. brought a steady stream of inquiries from people overseas. Nicholson kept every letter and compiled them in files by individual countries. As early as 1958, he shared his vision with Keith Funston, then Chairman of the New York Stock Exchange, who offered to throw his influence behind Nicholson's expansionist ideas. Funston, a booster of what he liked to call "the people's capitalism," had great success with the "Own Your Share of America" campaign, which encouraged individual investing by embracing the investment club idea.

As a part of that campaign, Funston had written a pamphlet about investment clubs. Because the U.S. State Department saw it as an excellent example of the American way of life, it was reproduced and sent to American embassies around the world. Embassy staffers and publicists in turn placed the story in the leading publications of many countries, which resulted in even more inquiries from potential investors all over the world. Among them was a letter from David W. Moate, an accountant in London who was interested in starting an investment club group in England. NAIC promptly provided him with information, and he quickly put together a group in London.

Moate was on fire for investment clubs. He traveled to the U.S. for NAIC's Ninth Annual convention in 1959, joining foreign delegates from New Zealand and Canada. Nicholson, realizing the time was ripe to expand in Europe, suggested that Moate invite other interested people to London in July of 1960 to found the World Federation of Investment Clubs.

The idea was an instant success. It proved to be so popular in the United States that NAIC chartered a plane to take over 80 people to Europe. Besides the U.S., Canada and England, representatives from Holland and New Zealand attended. The London Stock Exchange hosted the group. British government officials and economists addressed the delegates. At the closing banquet they dined at St. Stephan's Club, the official club for the House of Lords that is attached by tunnel to the Parliament Buildings.

Nicholson was practically treated as a Lord himself. But on the day that the new organization would select its leaders, Nicholson pulled O'Hara aside.

"When it comes time to discuss officers," he instructed, "I want to make sure that neither you nor anyone else in our delegation suggests my name. This is very important. If this is really to be a federation of clubs from around the world, it needs to be truly a world organization."

O'Hara agreed, but wondered why Nicholson was backing off from what seemed like his idea.

A few minutes later, as they filed into the banquet room for lunch, O'Hara was pulled away again, this time by several of the British members.

"Mr. O'Hara," the spokesman said, getting right to the point, "we see that you Americans comprise the largest delegation, and while we certainly do appreciate your expertise in this, we are concerned that you chaps will try to control this by having your Mr. Nicholson elected chairman."

Once again, O'Hara marveled at the wisdom of George Nicholson.

"I can assure you that is not going to happen," said O'Hara. "While we certainly see a strong relationship between all investment clubs everywhere, we have no intentions of dominating this federation."

The World Federation was designed for two main purposes.

The most important was to grow the investment club movement into a worldwide force for wider share ownership and the education of investors. The second was simply to exchange new ideas between different associations in different parts of the world. But from these two formalized goals, a third, informal purpose was achieved, particularly for the individual European investors who had long been ignored by their stodgy and ponderous financial bureaucracies. The Federation helped give the individual investor new political and economic clout as a sort of investor rights group. They planned to meet together in convention every three years.

George Nicholson couldn't have been happier. Back in Detroit, he took charge of building the investment club movement worldwide. Any contact from someone overseas seeking information was referred to Nicholson, who took a deep and personal interest in mentoring scores of new investment club members all over the globe. In the mid-sixties, this led to a trip around the world for Nicholson and his wife, Elizabeth, and several members of the Detroit Chapter of the English Speaking Union. Nicholson, met many old friends, people he had corresponded with for years.

Nicholson met and personally helped locals organize clubs in Ireland, Germany, Sweden, France, Israel, Belgium, Nigeria and Holland.

His travels and contact with investors around the world also gave him keen insight into the way economic and political developments in one country affect business all over the world.

In the late sixties, Nicholson picked up economic intelligence from abroad that he found chilling. Nicholson saw a growing financial crisis sweeping through Europe that was heading straight for America's shores.

The crisis had a one-word description.

Inflation.

It was out of control and about to collide head-on with NAIC.

The good times of financial growth, stability and booming membership rolls would come to a sudden and frightening end.

Staff Sergeant Tom O'Hara,
8th Air Force, 1942.

Tom in London, 1942.

Tom in Iceland, 1942.

Olga Florence O'Hara, 1889-1956.
Tom's mother.

Robert John O'Hara, 1884-1966.
Tom's father.

On the Au Sable with the Mutual Investment Club
of Detroit, 1954. *Standing: Justin Dunmire,
Tom Ohara, John Biscomb. Seated: Norman Hill
and Louis Rockwell.*

Robert and Olga O'Hara with grandsons
Thomas Jr. and Robert, 1955.

Casting off, 1958. *Tom O'Hara and
Louis Rockwell.*

Eleanor, Robert and Thomas Jr. O'Hara, 1959.

Measuring Growth — 5000 Clubs in 1955. *Tom O'Hara and George Nicholson.*

Mutual Investment Club of Detroit, 1959. *L-R: Tom O'Hara, Howard Wilson, Louis Rockwell, Arthur Baske, Robert Burger, John Biscomb, Fred Russell (founder), Leo Jacobson, Robert Pryor.*

World Federation of Investment Clubs, London, 1966. *L-R: Tom O'Hara, Eleanor O'Hara, William Hopkins, Great Britain, Penny DeSauter and Anthony DeSauter, Great Britain, Elizabeth and George Nicholson.*

World Federation of
Investment Clubs,
Netherlands, 1963.
*Eleanor O'Hara,
Lord Mayor of
Rotterdam, and
George Nicholson.*

World Federation of Investment
Clubs, London, 1966.
*George A. Nicholson, Jr.,
Chair of Closing Banquet.*

Tom and Eleanor O'Hara at World Federation of Investment Clubs, 1966.

On Tour With World Federation of Investment Clubs, Netherlands, 1963. *L-R: William Moate, Great Britain, John DeJonge, Netherlands Investment Club Association, unknown tourist, Tom O'Hara, and Tommy O'Hara (playing street organ).*

Family in Ireland, 1963. *Eleanor and boys with Aunt Margaret O'Hara.*

Kenneth Janke, "Mr. NAIC," 1970.

Thomas O'Hara, Jr., 1965.

Detroit Chapter of NAIC, 1968. *Jeanne Alfsen, Director, Eleanor and Tom O'Hara.*

Robert O'Hara, 1965.

NAIC's First Investment Show, 1966. *Tom O'Hara, Louise Rockewell, and George Nicholson implement Detroit City Council's action to rename Washington Boulevard for a week.*

U.S. Securities and Exchange
Commission's First National Individual
Investor Conference, 1984. *Tom O'Hara
and Arthur Levitt, SEC Chairman.*

NAIC Spring Rally, 1964.
Tom O'Hara.

Walker Cisler, CEO, Detroit Edison,
Recipient of Investment Award, 1965.
*Front row: Wagar Glas, Chairman of NAIC
Board, Walker Cisler, George Nicholson.
Back row: Tom O'Hara, Ken Janke,
Elaine Benson, Editor of Better Investing,
Bruce DeSpelder, Educational Director
Investment Education Institute.*

Youngest User of NAIC
Stock Selection Guide, 1976.
Susan Masten.

NAIC Board of Trustees, 1999. *Back Row L-R: Peggy Shmeltz, Lewis Rockwell, Tom O'Hara, Ken Janke, BethHamm, Lorrie Guston. Front Row L-R: Donald Danko, Robert Wynn, Lee Mumford, Ralph Seger, Jr., Richard Holthaus.*

New York Stock Exchange Annual Report, 1987. *Public director Tom O'Hara.*

NAIC Officers, 1999. *James Sobol, Karen Glidden, Bob O'Hara, Tom O'Hara, Donald Danko, Ken Janke.*

World Federation of Investment Clubs, 1969. *Tom O'Hara, John DeJonge, Netherlands, and Lorrie Gustin, Secretary.*

Chapter Six: Inflationary Lessons

"...surviving inflation..."

It all really started in the fifties, as the effects from the war eased and money began to flow again throughout the industrialized world.

It started slowly and mostly unnoticed for more than a decade. Gradual price hikes. Easier credit.

By the mid-sixties George Nicholson, along with a handful of economists, started to sound the alarm. Few people listened. What happened was a textbook definition of inflation: persistent increase in the level of consumer prices resulted in a persistent decline in the purchasing power of money, all of which was caused by an increase in available currency and credit beyond the proportion of available goods and services.

In 1968, it reached crisis stage in France. Premier Charles DeGaule was faced with severe labor unrest and attempted to solve the problem with an across-the-board ten percent wage increase. Workers around the world demanded similar actions, and corporations found the only way they could maintain labor peace was to keep raising wages. Each hike in worker pay led to consumer price hikes. Soon, both exceeded gains in productivity. Governments responded by printing more money.

The world economy began to take a severe downturn.

Investment clubs in the World Federation reported worrisome membership losses. Many clubs folded. For awhile, it wasn't so bad in the U.S., where the inflationary effects were felt the least.

Then came 1973. Almost overnight, the U.S. and the rest of the industrialized world was brought to its knees. Reflecting on the embargo a few years later, President Jimmy Carter called it "the moral equivalent of war."

Ironically, it was a real war half a world away that precipitated the worst domestic economic crisis the U.S. had felt since the Great Depression.

On Yom Kippur, the high Jewish Holy day, the Arab world attacked Israel. It became known as the Fourth Arab-Israeli War and it didn't last long. Israel quickly and handily beat off the attackers. But in retaliation for Western support of Israel during the brief conflict, the powerful Organization of Petroleum Exporting Countries (OPEC) imposed a sudden and absolute oil embargo.

The U.S., as Israel's most powerful supporter, saw the spigot from the oil-rich Arab nations completely shut off. Oil prices skyrocketed from $4.50 to twelve dollars per barrel.

There were no alternatives, for the U.S./OPEC cartel members controlled more than three-fourths of the world's oil reserves, providing forty percent of the world's supply.

Panic gripped the nation. Almost overnight, blocks-long lines formed at gasoline stations. Petroleum was rationed. The President went on television and asked citizens not to display Christmas lights that season. Even Las Vegas dimmed the lights on its glitzy casinos.

Emergency legislation enforced price controls.

The devastating effect of the oil shortage drove inflation into the double digits.

The individual investor was hit particularly hard.

For several years before the crisis, the U.S. and other major powers had tried to reduce inflation by a hastily-devised and erratically-imposed "stop-go" economic policy.

First, the governments tried to "stop" inflation by raising interest rates to slow business. The hope was that this would relieve inflationary pressures.

And it appeared to work. At first.

Then, as business responded to the higher interest rates and the economy cooled, the government reversed its position and suddenly lowered interest rates until economic growth started again.

Then it would impose another "stop" by raising rates again.

For several years before the oil crisis, this economic roller coaster ride caused major governments to jump back and forth from a "stop" or a "go" attitude towards business. Sometimes governments in Europe would be in a "stop" mode, while the U.S. and other nations were in the "go" phase.

The confusing and constantly changing policies devastated shareholders, as wild fluctuations in their holdings caused by the "stop-go" policies alternately pushed stock prices down and then pulled them back up. It became increasingly difficult for shareowners to follow NAIC recommendations on investing in good management because stock prices were suddenly being affected more by the capricious actions of the government, than the more measurable managerial decisions of the company.

Many investors just bailed out of the market. They quit investing, moving their money out of stocks and into Certificates of Deposit, savings and money market accounts.

When the oil shortages hit in the fall of 1973, over fourteen thousand investment clubs belonged to NAIC and a total of forty employees worked out of its Royal Oak headquarters.

The worldwide economic downturn accelerated the loss of membership in the organization. The number of member clubs plummeted to six thousand. And the number of fulltime NAIC employees was down to fifteen. Where before, bags full of mail were delivered every day to the headquarters, by 1975 sometimes so little mail came in that it was all processed and answered before noon. But that was only the beginning. The public's interest in stocks declined until mid-1983. NAIC's membership had dropped to 3,200 clubs and only six employees remained with the organization.

Attendance at NAIC conventions and conferences around the country plummeted. People bailed out of the market in droves.

The Association barely hung on and soon found itself unable to meet expenses.

The saving grace was that NAIC owned the building it occupied. Janke and O'Hara consolidated all of the operations into a small portion of the building. Then they portioned it off and rented out space to other people. The local union for Post Office workers rented about a third of the space. A cousin of Janke's wife Sally was a manufacturer's representative and leased out another section. A man who framed pictures rented a few other rooms. In the basement space formerly used by the NAIC mail room, a local candy company set up a packaging center, receiving shipments of bulk candy and then boxing them up for resale to its customers. The offices never smelled so good.

The rental income was a great boon to NAIC.

That, and the continuing sense of mission that drove George Nicholson, Tom O'Hara and Ken Janke.

"History tells us that this is temporary," said Nicholson to O'Hara during one of the lowest times. "As difficult as this may be to experience at this particular time, there are great lessons to be learned here. The underlying principles that have guided us these many years are just as valid as they ever were. In fact, if we learn the lessons this situation can teach us, we can help the individual investor to emerge stronger and more financially stable than ever before."

George Nicholson had been a student of economic and inflationary forces for many years. He decided that he needed to spell out the inflationary lessons as both an encouragement to investors going through the dark days of the seventies but also as a guide to new investors who he was sure would encounter a similar time of runaway inflation in the future.

Nicholson knew that history, indeed, does repeat itself. Thus he came up with a dozen guiding principles that, during times of inflation, would stand the test of time. Over many nights he wrote them all down. NAIC printed them in a folder "Twelve Lessons in Inflation," and distributed them in NAIC's *Better Investing* magazine.

Lesson 1. While the climate may appear bad for stocks, do not let your money be idle. Search out and hold the strongest companies.

"Investors in the United States are generally more ignorant on how to invest during a period of inflation than their European friends," Nicholson wrote. "The German inflation of 1924 and the French inflation of 1926, together with World War II inflations, provided them with a decisive margin of experience. That is why foreign purchases of common stocks were so heavy in 1975, while American investors were selling."

How do you win the battle of investing during inflation?

Nicholson answered by quoting Douglas MacArthur, who was once asked about the fine points of strategy in fighting a battle. MacArthur said: "You fight like the dickens until the battle is won."

Nicholson said: "This is good advice for investors. Don't be complacent and don't let your cash lie inactive. Keep on investing in common stocks until the battle is won." (The Mutual Investment Club of Detroit entered the great period of inflation with $500,000. That sum declined to $220,000. But the club kept applying NAIC principles and at the end of the inflationary period came out with $1,400,000.)

Lesson 2. Survivability is an important factor during inflation. Pick companies with strong survivability characteristics.

"The absolute key to inflation investing," said Nicholson, "is survival of the investment. A good company that is strong on management, demonstrates an ability to responsibly handle its finances and has stable, effective business principles, has a high probability of surviving.

"Avoid companies with a low probability of survival in your inflation investing," he suggested. "When choosing investments during times of inflation, rate survival probability at the top, at least until inflation is under control."

111

Lesson 3. Recognize the type of inflation that is occurring and choose companies capable of meeting its problems.

Nicholson's studies helped him identify several different types of inflation, and several different causes. Among the types he wanted investors to understand were "printing press" inflations, "cost-push" inflations and "government generated" inflations.

The 1924 German inflation following World War I was of the "printing press" type, he said. It was fast. A little girl's ten pfennig magazine rose to 200,000 marks from January to August. Soon the magazine was printing money for the government. Money became worthless.

The inflation in France that came when DeGaulle settled his political crisis in 1968 with a ten percent wage boost and the one created when OPEC quadrupled the price of oil were of the "cost-push" type.

The continuous efforts by the U.S. government to control the economy with deficit spending, and stimulation of the money supply during the seventies was a glaring example of "government-generated" inflation.

With each kind of inflation, Nicholson saw different implications for the investor.

"In a 'printing press' type of inflation," he said, "the company which has a high percentage of tangible and saleable assets is in a better position. That is, a scrap metal dealer would be able to price his assets upward as inflation intensified. In the other two types of inflation, stocks of companies with strong management skills enabling them to survive economic storms should be more valuable to investors."

Being able to identify the type and cause of inflation was critical, he said.

"Don't be fooled by changes in inflationary conditions. Choose the companies you invest in with a thought towards their ability to adjust to that type of inflation."

Lesson 4. Management, as always, is vitally important. Make sure management passes all of the tests in the Stock Selection Guide with top grades.

During inflation, wrote Nicholson, there is a premium on investing in companies having a chief executive officer with near fortune-telling abilities. "He must not only be a good manager under ordinary business conditions, but must have the skills and imagination to bring the corporation through the extreme turbulence of inflation."

To illustrate, Nicholson noted that a German lamp manufacturer received his biggest order in 1923. He found he had lost half his capital when delivery was made six months later in the midst of the 1924 inflation because replacing inventory would cost more than he received for his product. It was only then that he realized how important it was to properly price and maintain his inventories. "He survived by taking orders payable in American money and watching carefully the quality of his outstanding receivables," Nicholson noted.

The management skills Nicholson said were most needed to survive inflation are tight control of inventories and receivables, avoidance of loans that may come due when cash is short, pricing to cover costs, and ability to avoid dilution of the stockholders' equity by having to sell stock or a division of the business to survive.

Expansion, he said, is never advised in extreme inflations.

"Buy stocks only in companies that have inflation-minded managements who are perceptive of trends and who have an instinct for self-preservation," he said. "Don't buy stocks in companies whose managements are operating under 'business as usual' practices."

Lesson 5. Honest accounting is very important in inflationary periods. Be sure profits are coming from the operation of the business, not from price or inventory inflation.

After selecting an adequately managed company, Nicholson said successful inflation investors should remember that a coin has two sides. "Keep this in mind when the subject of inflation accounting is considered," he cautioned.

One side of the coin was well known to financial analysts and investors. Depreciation, based on book costs, was obviously not adequate to cover replacements at inflated prices, he said. Tied to this are the fallacy of inventory profits created by inflation.

"Companies can go broke paying taxes and dividends out of false profits."

But Nicholson said it was equally important to turn the coin over and see what was really there. "For companies that stay in business, any assets have years more of productive usefulness. These old machines will earn increased profits, if products are raised in price to match the inflation. Moreover, when new equipment with greater productive efficiency replaces old, profits per unit of output may offset any deficiency of depreciation. Stockholders may even gain, as old and new equipment are molded together to produce goods for sale at inflated price levels."

Inflation accounting statements should enable investors to weigh and better balance the over-statements of earnings in inflation against the under-statement of asset values, he suggested. "The latter should be the more important for investors in stocks of surviving companies, long term."

How should investors investigate the accounting figures? "Match over-statements of earnings against under-statement of assets in valuing common stocks," wrote Nicholson. "Don't fail to estimate potential stock values in the next prosperous period after inflation adjustments have taken place and new profit levels are attained."

Lesson 6. During inflation strong companies survive and grow even faster by taking over weak, poorly managed companies.

Nicholson had truly studied economic history well. He was convinced that inflations like the year-long German debacle of 1924 ended quickly because total inflation begets total unemployment. Bank deposits and paper money became valueless, although pennies retained their former value in the new money system because of the cost of replacement. The common good required that people accept restraints to get business going again.

The companies that survived, Nicholson noted, all survived by reason of tangible assets, ownership of foreign assets, valuable trademarks, or highly-proprietary "know-how" in manufacturing and distribution.

He told a lesson he learned from an executive of an American chemical company who was dispatched to Europe before World War II to study how corporations survived inflation. The executive told Nicholson that the key to surviving was creating a strategy for raising

114

money as prices soared and new financing was needed.

Nicholson concluded, inflation and expansion are much alike. Both need plenty of money to avoid insolvency. The problem was how to survive without diluting the stockholder's equity. The solution was to have assets, or divisions of the business, that could be sold to avoid bankruptcy. The financially and competitively strong corporations — whether big or small — survived best.

What about corporations that survive inflation?

"As inflation rages and abates, surviving companies inherit business from companies that fail," he said. "Some may double or triple their business in inflationary periods from the inheritance factor. New or used equipment, often bought at bankruptcy sales, sometimes is required for this expansion. Such bargains help offset depreciation deficiencies. They also raise the quality of future earnings."

Nicholson said investors should take advantage of this "inheritance factor" in inflation investing. "Don't invest in companies that lack survival characteristics or which dilute stockholder's equity substantially."

Lesson 7. Where government is conducting an inflation control "stop-go" movement, recognize this as a time not of fear but a time for bargain hunting. Be sure you don't sell just as the shift to "go" is being made.

"Inflation-fighting by government is like slowing down an automobile on icy pavements. Put on the brakes. Take off the brakes before skidding badly. Repeat and repeat until inflation is slowed and stopped." That's how Nicholson described "stop-go" economic policies.

He described how the French government applied this technique in 1926 after seeing the disastrous German inflation of 1924. Nicholson's research concluded that the braking period can be maintained for about a year, while taking off the brakes may last for two years or more.

This type of inflation-fighting is what the big industrial nations used in Europe, Japan, and America during the seventies.

Investors, meanwhile, were told that stocks were a poor inflation hedge because stocks were lower in price when inflation was highest.

Nicholson strongly disputed such reasoning.

"Investors should have been told instead that inflation is a 'stop-go' operation, that any 'stop' operation hurts the price of stocks at least temporarily but that a controlled 'stop-go' operation is generally a safer type of depression than one which results from a collapsing boom. Instead of selling, stock holdings should be increased when the "go" phase begins."

Nicholson taught that investors needed to recognize the "stop" phase of "stop-go" as a time for bargain hunting among the stocks of large and small corporations with good potential for survival.

"Don't accept the propaganda gimmick that stocks are a poor inflation hedge and sell out just before the 'go' phase begins," he urged.

Lesson 8. Utilities are subject to "regulatory lag." Regulators often are late adjusting rates to inflation. This tends to make utilities excellent buys late in the inflation cycle.

Nicholson saw the advantages of utility stocks during inflation investing. Electricity is essential. Earnings power is generally of high quality, he said.

Utility stocks, though, can also have disadvantages. "These stocks suffer because of a phenomenon known in financial circles as 'regulatory lag.' Public service commissions are slow in adjusting utility rates to higher costs. This is particularly true of big city utilities."

Eventually, the political self-interest of the regulators usually corrected this situation. For example, he reported, French utility stocks in the 1926 inflation gained over one hundred percent, registering one of the best performances on the Bourse. This was no miracle. Many French municipalities owned stock in their utility companies. They opted for higher dividends to balance budgets rather than low rates for electric users. "Being owners they knew their costs and the need for recovering them quickly," he explained.

Nicholson taught that in America, the standard of intellectual honesty solves the regulatory problem in time. "Long range self-interest dictates political fairness because states that treat utilities unfairly lose credit standing and their ability to attract new industry."

"Regulatory lag" in raising rates varies from state to state. The fairer, prompter acting states were the first to attract investors. The laggards had to follow or accept the consequences of reduced employment opportunities, possible brown-outs, and curtailed services.

Thus, Nicholson said, investing to take advantage of "regulatory lag" had advantages in high quality and income, and good probabilities of appreciation. He saw utilities as an attractive total return investment in the "go" phase of "stop-go" inflation fighting and a fine medium for dollar cost averaging.

"Utility stocks of companies located in states regulated by public service commissions with established reputations for sound judgment and intellectual honesty, are attractive investments in the latter stages of inflation," Nicholson wrote. "Don't be fooled into thinking 'regulatory lag' is permanent."

Lesson 9. Inflation lag also takes place in stock prices. Put this lag to work for you in finding bargains.

"Regulatory lag" in utilities, said Nicholson, had a companion that relatively few investors knew about, namely "inflation lag" in stock prices.

"Inflation lag is deeply rooted in behavior patterns of investors," he wrote. "Whereas utility regulators are prodded by necessity to make inflation adjustments, most investors lack training in inflation investing, are scared and confused, and are hesitant to act to take advantage of 'inflation lag' in stock prices."

Often opportunities were greatest when investors were in doubt about depreciating money, investments, and even jobs. They heard that the "system" no longer worked, that stocks were no inflation hedges at all and they worried and sold off or did nothing. The investor thus was influenced by bits of trivia and not by the big picture.

But when the "go" phase of "stop-go" inflation fighting got underway, it was easier to see the big picture. "As adjustments to inflation progresses, normal profit margins produce higher earnings per share. Investors become 'believers,' businesses that survive inflation become growth companies, and speculation eventually develops increased price-earnings multiples and wipes out 'inflation lag.'"

Thus every investor needed to become familiar with and use "inflation lag" in inflation investing. "Don't miss the catch up phases in stock prices which may lag by several years behind the passing of the greatest danger period of inflation," he cautioned.

Lesson 10. During periods of high inflation there is a temptation to move into bonds paying ten percent or more. The most important task is always to protect principal. This means being at least seventy percent in stock.

Nicholson felt investors were easily confused by interest rates during periods of inflation-fighting by the governments.

"Probably the most common mistake is rushing into eight to ten percent bonds to meet the cost of living and selling stocks because they are down," he said. "Years hence you may be saying 'that's how I made my big mistake. I opted for more income instead of more principal.'"

It wasn't just individual investors who fell into this trap, he said. Money managers too, made mistakes on interest rates. They tried to out-guess the Federal Reserve Bank by speculating on short-term shifts from bonds to stocks and back again. Nicholson knew that few could beat the house.

Stick with stocks, he said. It was Nicholson's experience over the years that owning stocks of well-managed, growing companies was always likely to beat the eight to ten percent interest offered on bonds and preferred stocks. Playing interest rate roulette with the Federal Reserve was seldom profitable.

"Protection of principal against inflation should be primary and income secondary," he wrote. "Don't goof by snapping at the bait of high or fluctuating interest rates."

Lesson 11. Comparison is a stock selection method that always works. In inflation times stick with basic comparisons and don't venture into the unknown.

Comparison was a major technique of financial analysis. Industries, companies, stocks and bonds were compared to find the "best" values. Rates of sales and earnings growth, pre-tax profit margins, and earnings on invested capital were compared in selecting lists of growth stocks.

However, said Nicholson, if the head of research at a major brokerage house asked for the best inflation stocks, his analysts all might come up with different lists. For example, spending more on research and development would likely reduce profit margins and earnings on invested capital. Therefore, a stock might be rejected on a "growth" list, but qualify for an "inflation" list, because of increasing assets, product lines, and awareness of the importance of financial position.

Other inflation comparisons and judgments would cause some analysts to favor the low dividend pay-out companies; or firms able to expand internally; or managements skilled in making successful acquisitions. Still others would avoid companies with short-term debts and high risks; while others would make their choice comparing cost of sales ratios and pricing.

Those were all valid comparisons. And there were more. But the point was, said Nicholson, the investor must have objective facts on which to make comparisons, not hunches or theories. That means investors must do their homework.

"The key is to select companies that can survive financial strains, have managements capable of inheriting business successfully from those that fail, and stocks that should attract investors when inflation lag catches up," he said. "It is better to emphasize companies and de-emphasize industries in inflation investing. Also, medium-sized and smaller companies may be the better inflation investments."

Nicholson said comparisons must be apples to apples, not apples to oranges. "Make relevant comparisons," he urged.

Lesson 12. Remember the investment rule stated by Justice Putnam in 1830. "Do what you will, the capital is at risk. Observe how men of prudence, discretion and intelligence manage their own affairs in regard to the permanent disposition of their funds, considering the possible income as well as the probable safety of the capital to be invested."

Inflation was tricky. Nicholson told the NAIC members that there was no absolute answer to inflation investing. The Prudent Man Rule decision in 1830 by Justice Samuel Putnam of Massachusetts dealt with a case about the investment of trust funds. But the old jurist's words had been tested by time and survived many inflations in many places.

119

Nicholson, noting the words "permanent"..."income"..."safety"... thought Putnam would have made a great NAIC member. What the Justice was saying, said Nicholson, was look ahead to future purchasing power. Short-term speculation was obviously to be avoided.

It was right out of the NAIC principles.

"The key to everything is the 'permanent disposition' guidance in the Prudent Man Rule," wrote Nicholson. "Don't fail to use prudence, discretion and intelligence during inflation, always with longer term in mind."

The worldwide economic downturn occasioned by out of control inflation and the 1973 oil crisis tested the wisdom of George Nicholson and NAIC like nothing else. None of the Association officers or members who stayed the course and kept following those principles would ever wish to go through it again. But, as the economy began to turn around in the eighties and the principles proved correct, the losses slowly evaporated. Membership began to build once again. Then it boomed. Soon, the Association reclaimed the space it had rented out in the headquarters building. They hired new employees.

In the end, despite the worry and tension and belt-tightening that tough economic times occasioned, NAIC emerged stronger and more focused than ever. The lessons Nicholson so tenaciously taught stood the test of time.

Time does, however, change things. And as NAIC moved into the eighties, things started to change at breakneck speed. In 1982, the annual NAIC convention in Philadelphia saw an increase in the number of attendees and exhibitors, for the first time since the Chicago convention in 1965.

Deep recession had broken and, slowly at first but then in an ever-increasing torrent of letters, phone calls and favorable media stories, everything turned around. NAIC rehired employees and rebuilt. Membership rolls grew again.

New clubs and new members joined so fast that new tools were needed.

Those tools came in the form of the personal computer and special investment club software.

It really began in the mid-sixties with the electronic calculator. Prior to that, the NAIC Stock Selection Guide, and many of the other analytical research steps were performed by pencil and paper, a tedious process. When the first desktop electronic calculators came on the market, many a club treasurer hailed them as accounting lifesavers. By the seventies every club and most members had invested in a handheld calculator, an invention that drastically reduced the time required to complete NAIC forms.

The Association itself had begun to experiment with computers as far back as 1966. Ken Janke, in his continuing quest to streamline operations at NAIC headquarters, searched for a way to notify club members when it was time to renew. In a conversation one day with Tom O'Hara, Janke heard how computers at the Detroit Board of Education helped to keep track of board finances and personnel. Janke found a Detroit computer service company that agreed to convert the entire NAIC membership rolls to computer punch cards. The new automated process brought an immediate decrease in costs.

The "computer revolution" began with the introduction of the personal computer in the early eighties, a time that coincided with the beginning of what would become the longest sustained boom market the nation has ever experienced. The early machines, from Apple and IBM, were big, bulky and balky. Yet compared to pencil and paper, and even the calculator, they made it a breeze to fill out the Stock Selection Guide.

As PC use grew among NAIC members, so did CompuServe. Founded in 1969 as a computer time-sharing service, the Columbus, Ohio-based CompuServe pioneered the online service industry. In 1979, CompuServe became the first service to offer electronic mail capabilities and technical support to personal computer users.

It didn't take long for NAIC members to start sharing SSG reports and stock analysis by e-mail and during the CompuServe forums, or discussion groups, started by a member named Ed Chiampi. Chiampi was an evangelist for NAIC and computer-assisted investing. At conventions and club meetings around the country, people exchanged printouts of CompuServe forum messages and e-mails. By 1982, several hundred people regularly checked into the forum, extolling the virtues of personal computers and investing. Chiampi began writing a column on computers for *Better Investing* magazine and, in 1984, formed the NAIC Computer Group. Some 550 members came together for the first session.

"Remember, the computer will save time and report your figures accurately," wrote Chiampi in a September 1984 column. "But you should not ask it to make your decisions."

The PC, he kept telling everyone, was not a magic wand. "Think of your computer as a tool," he wrote in 1985.

Joe Craig, another NAIC computer pioneer, started checking into the CompuServe forums. So did Dick Kenfield. Both would later become presidents of the NAIC Computer Group. Other members like Dick Dwyer, Liz Hart, Herb Barnett, Nancy Isaacs, David Elias, Nancy Crays and Doug Gerlach drifted in. Soon, the NAIC forum on CompuServe was one of the service's most popular destinations as volunteers patiently answered questions from new investors, blending computers with NAIC's investment principles and stock study procedures. Online investment clubs sprang up in which none of the members ever met face to face. They simply communicated online.

Specialized software that tracked performance developed, too, first in the old DOS and Apple formats, then for Windows and MacIntosh. The EvalForm and the Stock Selection Guide programs opened the doors to common stock investing for more people than ever before. By making investing more fun, more accurate, more enabling and less time consuming, computers soon added a new dimension to long-term investing, helping clubs and individuals all around the world.

In June of 1995, the Computer Group volunteers won approval from the NAIC board of directors to develop an official site on the World Wide Web. Registered as better-investing.org, it took its name from the very slick and popular magazine, the flagship of the NAIC publications.

Today the Web site records a million visits each month. On the site, visitors can learn about NAIC, read investing articles, find local clubs and classes and sign up for an e-mail discussion group called the I-Club-List. The I-Club has thousands of members, and on any given day generates as many as 150 messages about investments, the market's ups and downs and tricks and tips to using the NAIC investment tools.

Women have always been a big part of NAIC.

In 1988, NAIC found that slightly over thirty-seven percent of NAIC Clubs were comprised of all female members. About thirty-five percent had mixed members. Ten years later, the percentage of women members totaled nearly sixty-eight percent.

The all-women clubs also have out-performed all-male clubs, too.

In 1998, the average compounded annual lifetime earnings rate for all-female clubs was 23.8%, compared to a rate of 19.2% for all male clubs. The earnings rate for mixed gender clubs was 21.4%.

NAIC officials saw these clear trends and wondered why. They began asking questions, hoping that the success tactics could be applied by all members.

Several reasons for the better success by women quickly emerged.

For one thing, the information showed that new women's clubs tended to more closely follow NAIC's investing philosophy and guidelines for setting up and running an effective investment club, analyzing stocks and managing a portfolio. For another, women's clubs typically followed a buy-and-hold strategy when buying quality stocks for the long-term. Thirdly, Tom O'Hara and Ken Janke would often tell the press when asked about this phenomenon, Association records clearly showed that women's clubs were not quick to buy or sell a stock on the up or down price movement of a stock or current economic or stock market changes.

"Women's clubs tend to be more willing to ride out the rough times to realize a profit on an investment," O'Hara frequently said.

There were other factors. Women, NAIC officers observed, were traditionally the purchasers of many household goods and services. They were more in the habit of looking for quality goods and services for a fair price, the exact goals of NAIC when selecting a stock. As the most frequent "buyers," women tended to be keenly aware of quality, fairly priced and competitive goods and services in the marketplace, including the companies that produce the goods and

123

services. Janke observed this with his own wife, Sally, who ran her own investment club and frequently held investing seminars for NAIC members.

"This valuable knowledge that women have translates directly to stock investing — looking for quality, growing, competitive companies that are available at a good price," noted a section about women investors on the NAIC Web page. "The best research for finding good companies to invest in is out in the marketplace — experiencing the company's products and services firsthand."

Another factor was the substantial increase in the number of women entering the workforce since 1980, which increased their own personal wealth. More women in the workplace became aware of investing through company-offered savings and retirement plans such as a 401k, IRA, ESOP, pension plans or other programs. In addition, because of societal trends, more women found themselves as the sole provider for their family. Women, NAIC learned, quickly understood and committed to the principle of building investments for future needs, whether retirement, children's education, or the financial effects of the death of a spouse.

Across the country as the nation began to emerge from the economic recession of the seventies, women embraced the financial benefits of long-term investing in stocks. Tens of thousands found participation in an investment club a sound way to gain knowledge about investing and to help secure their financial future.

"Women's clubs often look at a broad picture of the prospects of a valuable growth company or the general trends in the stock market," said the NAIC Web page. "Women's clubs may not become too focused or "drowned" in the many specific technical and financial details that may detract from a company's fundamental potential or long-term future growth prospects."

NAIC experience showed that women's clubs tended to focus on the fundamentals of a company, such as looking at management's performance and the characteristics of the industry a company operates within.

"This broad-based, fundamental approach clearly follows NAIC's investment philosophy, which has proven to produce successful investors over the long-term," said NAIC.

It would be a women's investment club in a tiny little town in Illinois that would give NAIC its greatest notoriety.

Mostly widowed grandmothers comprised the club that gathered in the basement of the Lutheran Church in Beardstown, Illinois. Each contributed one hundred dollars to get organized and then agreed to kick in twenty-five dollars a month.

They would become, perhaps, the most famous group of grandmothers the country has ever seen.

Chapter Seven: A Gathering of Friends

eardstown, Illinois was a tiny agricultural town of 6,200, a forty-five minute drive west from the capital of Springfield. It was a quiet town, the quintessential Midwest farming community where the largest industry was a pork slaughterhouse and its biggest claim to fame was that it was the site of a Lincoln-Douglas debate in 1858.

But that was before the Beardstown Ladies.

The Beardstown Ladies officially began in the basement of the First Lutheran Church, October, 1983 as The Beardstown Business and Professional Women's Investment Club. Elizabeth (Betty) Sinnock, a local banker at the Havana National Bank, had read an article on the

National Association of Investors Corporation, sent away for literature and recruited fifteen of her friends to start the club.

The women, mostly seniors, grandmothers and widows were close friends. Active in church and community affairs they religiously met the first Thursday of the month, year after year, and they found that following NAIC investment principles, doing the Stock Selection Guide studies and reinvesting all their profits brought an impressively growing portfolio.

By 1987, the club's returns caught the attention of NAIC headquarters and it was named an All Star club, a prestigious designation granted only to the best performing clubs. And so it went, year after year. Betty Sinnock became one of the best-known NAIC volunteers in the Midwest, teaching numerous NAIC six-week-long stock selection courses at the local college and tirelessly helping anyone and everyone who called with questions.

The club became so successful, in fact, that in 1995, it published a book called *The Beardstown Ladies Common Sense Investment Guide*. This instant best seller made the Beardstown Ladies become overnight celebrities, appearing on national television shows and in scores of major newspapers. "With a portfolio worth more than $90,000 and an impressive average return of twenty-three percent, the Beardstown Ladies' Investment Club has the secret recipe for investment success. These sixteen women have been outperforming mutual funds and professional money managers three to one; now they reveal their secrets," read a promotional blurb from their publisher.

Newsweek Magazine delivered a glowing review. "Looking for proof that you needn't work on Wall Street to beat the market? Meet the Beardstown Ladies...The book provides good advice to novice stock-pickers."

So did *The New York Times*: "The book details a highly thoughtful approach to picking stocks that puts many Wall Street experts to shame."

Beardstown landed on the map. Tourists drove down from Chicago with copies of the book for the Ladies to sign. The Chamber of Commerce offered directions to the church. A second book, *The*

Beardstown Ladies Stitch in Time Guide to Growing Your Nest Egg, became another best seller. A video followed, *Cooking Up Profits on Wall Street*, which combined investment tips with the Ladies' home cooking recipes.

The Beardstown Ladies were the toast of the financial world. Maxine Thomas, a seventy-five year old widow, received a half dozen marriage proposals, one from as far away as Australia. But none of the women let the fame go to their heads. In fact, just the opposite occurred.

In every interview, there was a strong sense of grateful modesty. "We're using the gifts God gave us," Maxine would say, "and we want to share what we learn." Her friend, Carnell Korsmeyer, put it this way: "God made us people of choice. Learning to make the right choices is expressive of our faith."

For NAIC, the success of the Beardstown Ladies brought a huge increase in investment clubs. At every opportunity, the women would sing the praises of NAIC.

"A club is a good way to learn," Carnell told interviewers. "Everyone shares in the work, and there isn't lots of risk. It's good for club members to have diverse backgrounds, but it's important that they share a similar philosophy about investing. You need to know what you're comfortable risking."

Their advice was straight out of NAIC bulletins. "We call ourselves conservative," said Carnell in a newspaper story distributed across the world by the Associated Press. "We invest for the long term, so we pick growth companies. And we don't jump in and out."

The story concluded: "The Beardstown Ladies don't bail out when a stock drops; they see that as a chance to buy more stock at bargain rates. They say, 'Have faith and remember: even with all the drops, over the last century the market's general direction has been up.' To those who say, 'I don't have enough money to invest,' Carnell and Maxine both point out: 'One of our club members says we should pay ourselves first. When you get paid, set aside an amount to invest. You've worked for that money. Now make it work for you. The plan is more important than the amount. Just be sure to do it regularly."

In another interview, member Buffy Tillitt-Pratt described what common sense investing meant to the Beardstown Ladies: "We invest with our hearts, our eyes and our stomachs. We buy stocks from companies whose products we know and use. We add our own life experience to the analysis we do on a company before making decisions." Before investing in Wal-Mart stock, for example, the women checked out the local store to see how busy it was and what products it carried.

With publicity like this, it seemed as if the Beardstown Ladies and their solid, common sense Midwestern advice were destined to become investment world icons. The Walt Disney people even considered doing a movie about them.

But then everything changed.

Shane Tristch, a reporter at *Chicago Magazine*, did a careful financial analysis of the return on investments claimed by the Ladies. He found that the actual return from 1984-1993 was just 9.1 percent, far short of the 23.4% annualized returns that the club had promoted. It turned out that that 23.4% growth was a statement of returns for their 1991-1992 performance, not for the full decade. The Beardstown Ladies were as shocked as everyone else. They submitted the club books to a detailed audit by Price Waterhouse accounting firm. Auditors concluded the inflated earnings were the result of a data input error. In calculating their returns, the Ladies, it turned out, had counted the regular monthly dues they contributed over the decade, besides the stock dividends and increases in value.

It was a simple mistake.

But the financial press turned and pounced on the Beardstown Ladies like the hungry lions unleashed on Christians by the ancient Romans.

Time Magazine even ran a headline that said "Jail the Beardstown Ladies!"

Across the world, financial columnists and journalists discredited, poked fun and laughed at the Ladies they once praised. Movie plans were scuttled. Brokerage houses used the publicity to urge people to quit trying to do-it-themselves and instead rely on their high-priced advice.

In Beardstown, the Ladies were devastated. "We're just sick over this," said founder and treasurer Betty Sinnock, who attributed the mistake to an error in recording data in a computer program the club used to track their financial dealings. "The ladies were very concerned that the public would think we had purposely misrepresented results in any of our books," Sinnock said in a statement. "We shared this original rate of return in good faith and are terribly sorry for the error and any confusion it may have caused."

For weeks, the smug attacks continued.

The Ladies worried about what effect this would have on NAIC.

Betty Sinnock sent an explanation to NAIC's headquarters, asking that it be widely distributed.

"To all NAIC Treasurers," it read:

"With all the recent publicity that our club has gotten lately, I know that many NAIC Club Treasurers have wondered why we were so far off in reporting our return for the first ten years.

"Briefly, here's the story:

"In 1992 the club offered to buy the NAIC Club Accounting Software if I could get permission to use it on a computer at the bank since I didn't own a computer. I entered the data as of 12/31/91 and I thought I was inputting the data so the first eight years would be included in our returns. Because of this, when the computer showed an annual return for our members in 1993 of 23.4%, I thought it was for the first ten years and shared the information with the rest of the ladies and with the producer of our video which had recently been completed. We were very proud of what we thought we had done but we never intended to brag or boast about this.

"We have since learned that the 23.4% was for a two year period and not for the first ten years that we had always thought. We are truly sorry and pray that the people who have bought our books did so because they wanted to learn about investing in the market and not because the 23.4% was printed on the cover.

"In retrospect, we feel very foolish that we had not checked the figures for ourselves. If only I had taken the time to input all of our transactions when we got the computer program we would have had a true figure to report.

"The NAIC Accounting Software is a must for investment clubs if

131

it is used correctly. I encourage new clubs to get it as soon as possible. The distribution task at year-end alone is worth the money spent on the program.

"Sincerely, Betty Sinnock, Senior Partner, Beardstown Business and Professional Women's Club, AKA The Beardstown Ladies, 3/30/98."

Back in Michigan, at NAIC headquarters, officials anxiously watched the controversy over the Beardstown Ladies. Some braced for what they thought would be negative fallout from all the negative attention.

Surprisingly, it didn't happen.

Individual investors were not bailing out on the Ladies at all. Requests for information on how to set up a Beardstown-styled investment club continued to pour in to NAIC.

And then, perhaps picking up on an undercurrent of support building for the Ladies by individual investors, the popular Motley Fool personal finance Internet Web site (www.motleyfool.com) analyzed all the negative publicity and decided that maybe the sudden turn on the Ladies by the mainstream financial press wasn't warranted.

The Motley Fool review on the controversy found several points ignored in much of the criticism over the Ladies' admittedly sloppy bookkeeping.

"First, there's a little more context that the financial pages didn't offer," noted the Fool. "True, the Beardstowners racked up 9.1% gains versus 14.9% growth for the S&P 500 between 1984-1993. But the Beardstown Club actually has been in existence longer than the 10 years reported by most media organizations. Price Waterhouse's report included that, over the 14-year period of their existence, the Beardstown Ladies Club's compounded annual growth was 15.3% versus 17.2% for the S&P 500. Not better than an index fund, but not bad."

But there was more, said the Fool.

"Second, even though the Beardstown Ladies did measurably under-perform the market between 1984 and 1993, their total savings rate showed annualized growth much higher than that. No, the total growth rate doesn't reflect the return on invested capital...but it does speak to the accumulation of wealth—the larger aim of most investors. As anyone who comes to this forum knows, adding new savings to your investment portfolio every week, month, or year can have dramatic effects on a patient plan to build wealth.

"Third, hey, when do we audit the businesses that make enormous amounts of money off the individual investor, now that we've put the Beardstown Ladies through the ringer? There has never been a public audit of the performance of full-service brokers in America, even as they generate a few billion dollars more business than the Beardstown Ladies each year. If your financial advisor, planner, broker, consultant, or swami can't provide you with your annual rates of return—after deducting all fees, costs, expenses, commissions, production credits, whatever—and if that consultant is unwilling to then compare your returns to market average for you, you're not being served.

"Fourth, mutual funds are required to publicly state audited returns in America. And, over the past five years, 91% of them have under-performed the S&P 500—before even factoring in the biting tax costs from the high turnover ratio at most funds. Likewise, more than 75% of this trillion-dollar industry under-performed the market during the 14-year history of the Beardstown Ladies Investment Club; certainly more than half did worse than the Ladies after subtracting out fees and taxes. (The Ladies buy and hold.)"

The Motley Fool article concluded by suggesting, in effect, that the fickle financial press pick on someone their own size.

"While our largest financial institutions are regulated, their perfor-mance hasn't really been scrutinized by the financial press yet. A Fool wonders, for example, why the mainstream media hasn't brought the same imagination and zeal exhibited in their coverage of the Beardstowners (*"Jail the Beardstown Ladies!"*) to even just a very general review of our nation's big-money institutions. America would learn some great lessons if the press regularly just scratched the surface on the performance of credit cards, financial planners, mutual funds, home equity loans, whole-life insurance, et cetera."

Back in Beardstown, the Beardstown Ladies tightened up their accounting and, after apologizing for any confusion, kept right on meeting. Their bottom line message, they kept saying, was about learning how to invest in the stock market.

"We've always thought that our purpose was to educate and we didn't mean to mislead anyone," explained Carnell Korsmeyer when a *Chicago Tribune* reporter interviewed her a few months after the controversy. "I guess I thought when it happened, it would have an adverse impact on book sales and speaking engagements, but it hasn't."

The Ladies continued to be booked weeks in advance at clubs throughout the region, talking and teaching NAIC principles. At least a half dozen other movie offers came in since the discovery of the bookkeeping snafu. The ladies turned them all down saying they were more interested in educating, than entertaining.

Some of the people who knew him best think George Nicholson was a soothsayer. His keen analytical mind and rapid interest in world politics and its effect on the economy proved right time after time.

In November 1987, writing in NAIC's *Better Investing* magazine, Nicholson predicted:

"The remaining years of the twentieth century — logically and without euphoria over small signs — should establish new investment records based on growing global businesses. Business should be steadier because, in my view, growth and risk-reward ratios are improving as 2000 A.D. approaches and are better than they have been in the previous eighty-seven years."

Nicholson wrote that prediction after a very busy six months spent traveling the world and learning about what would later become known as the global economy. In July of that year, he had led an NAIC People-to-People Investment Management Delegation to China and personally met with the Vice Premier, Zhang Jing Fu, who literally ran the financial affairs of a nation. It was supposed to be a two-minute conversation, according to the Vice Premier's handlers. They had been very clear about that. Zhang Jing Fu was too busy to give up any more time. They told Nicholson to "keep your remarks brief."

Nicholson stuck to the script. He explained that the delegation had come so they could better understand China and help its leaders with understanding investment. The group included officials of funds managing tens of billions of dollars as well as investment educators of small investors. The group included people skilled at the university level in teaching investment management and in stockholder relations.

"All our people came of their own free will because, like people all over the world, investors wanted to buy Chinese securities," Nicholson said.

"That's what they all say," said Zhang. Flattery was nice. He held Nicholson's eyes, waiting for his reply. The two minutes was up. Nicholson didn't want to violate protocol but he did indeed want to respond. The interpreter nodded to go ahead.

"People like the Chinese character and want to invest in it," Nicholson said. "Besides, you should know that in every two hundred and fifty million people, there is a certain amount of genius. China, with its one billion citizens, has five times the genius of most other nations. That's worth investing in."

It was typical Nicholson. Brilliant. To the point. Provocative. The Vice Premier was intrigued, and he was clearly thinking about what Nicholson said as the interpreter translated.

Nicholson couldn't help himself. He stuck his index finger near Zhang's nose and said "you are a genius." Great laughter followed, and the conversation ran fifty minutes, instead of two.

The world was changing. Russia and China dramatically shifted their economies toward more market orientation, utilizing modern banking and security markets to speed industrialization.

Then came "Black Monday," the largest stock-market drop in Wall Street history, on October 19, 1987. The Dow Jones Industrial Average plunged 508.32 points, losing 22.6% of its total value. That fall far surpassed the one-day loss of 12.9% that began the great stock market crash of 1929 and foreshadowed the Great Depression. The Dow's 1987 fall also triggered panic selling and similar drops in stock markets worldwide. And it came at the end of a five year bear market that had seen the Dow average rise from 776.92 points in August, 1982 to a high of 2,722.42 points in August, 1987. For months, the financial press reported gloom and doom, much of it predicting a worldwide depression.

Nicholson was not even the least bit concerned by "Black Monday." It was a minor blip, he said. Nothing to panic about. Besides, his extensive travels had convinced him that the changing world was about to cause a boom in personal investing.

"In my opinion we are putting together the new world economy of the future — stock markets and political and economic institutional practices that will dominate the next century," he wrote in March of 1988.

How right he was. By the end of 1989, the losses from Black Monday were all made up. And in the nineties, nearly everyone became an investor.

"The opportunities that lie ahead for global growth and prosperity are as enormous as ever," he wrote in 1994 as the market really began to take off. "We are experiencing one of the most constructive periods in history."

Over the next six years, the market would grow at rates close to, or sometimes over, twenty percent. Nicholson watched with unbridled joy as millions of everyday investors flocked to the market.

The sudden increase in personal investing was aided by the development and widespread use of the personal computer and fueled by the explosion of the Internet. Technology stocks doubled, tripled, quadrupled in price. Fifty million people were regularly investing in stocks and mutual funds. More than 700,000 people belonged to NAIC investment clubs. CNBC television, the Bloomberg Report, Money Line and a host of other popular mass-market television investment channels and programs whipped up massive public interest. Internet Web sites like NAIC's www.better-investing.org drew tens of thousands of devoted and regular users able to exchange accurate financial information and educational tips with the click of a mouse.

George Nicholson enjoyed the satisfaction of knowing he was right. He saw his dream come true.

However, he died before he saw just how right he was. The economic good times he predicted turned into the most sustained and powerful bull market the world had ever seen.

George Nicholson passed away quietly and comfortably in his

Grosse Pointe Park, Michigan, home on July 21, 1996 of congestive heart failure. He was eighty-eight years old. His last wish was that, instead of memorials and flowers, contributions be made to NAIC investment education programs to train future investors.

Tom O'Hara wrote the eulogy for his dear friend. It appeared as an editorial headlined "He gave his Mind and Heart to Investment Clubs and Individual Investors," and appeared in the September 1996 edition of *Better Investing*.

"George was a visionary and architect of mass investor education," O'Hara wrote. "He saw investment education as the way to a better life for tens of millions of individuals, and as a way to build and strengthen our economic system. George was very far-sighted. He planned in terms of years and lifetimes."

Tom O'Hara's tribute to his mentor and friend coincided with a major change in his own life.

On September 30, 1996, O'Hara relinquished many of his day-to-day activities at NAIC to the man who was his next best friend, Ken Janke, who became President and CEO. O'Hara was not retiring. Far from it. He would continue to be Chairman of the NAIC Board of Trustees and have an office in the NAIC headquarters in Madison Heights. But O'Hara would concentrate more on broad items of policy and development instead of operations.

The Mutual Investment Club of Detroit celebrated its sixtieth anniversary in September, 1999 at the City Club in Nashville. Two bus loads of members, their relatives and a select group of friends made the twenty minute drive downtown from the sprawling Opryland Hotel and convention complex, where NAIC was holding its forty-ninth annual Congress and Expo. NAIC's theme for the last such gathering of the twentieth century was "Investing for the New Millennium."

On this Friday night, as a new millennium and a new century was about to dawn, the Mutual Investment Club of Detroit was still going strong, more than sixty years after it began.

When it started in 1939, its dozen members began with a total contribution of ten dollars each, for initial assets of $120.

After all those years, through bear markets and bull markets, through World War II, and regional conflicts like Korea, Vietnam, Desert Storm, through ten U.S. Presidents, through budget deficits and budget surpluses, through liberal and conservative legislatures, and all of the sweeping political and cultural changes a half-century plus a decade had brought about, the club proved beyond a shadow of a doubt how the NAIC principles will always be successful over the long haul.

It took a while. But by 1946, club members had collectively invested $5,088, and those holdings were worth $15,347. In Nashville at the sixtieth anniversary dinner, several member recalled with amusement how there had been talk, back in 1946, of cashing in the funds and making off with the tripled profit. Saner heads fortunately prevailed. In 1952, those assets had doubled to over $30,000. Just three years later, thanks to the strong and steady economic policies of the Eisenhower administration, they had doubled again to over $60,000.

In 1959, the assets more than doubled, to $160,000. In 1965, $240,000. Richard Nixon was elected President in 1968 on a promise to get the country out of Vietnam. The club reached the doubling point of $480,000 in 1969, the year following the 1968 French Upheaval, which brought the cost-push inflation years into wage structures of all nations and produced unrest everywhere. The next doubling, in 1982, was $960,000 in the early years of the Reagan Administration. This was the Mutual Investment Club's longest doubling period. There was the confusion of Watergate, the use of confusion tactics in politics by the Carter Administration, and the culmination of world inflation that began in the 1960s. The club reached the $1,920,000 doubling point in 1987, despite eight withdrawals totaling $474,000.

On and on it went, the club doubling in value just about every five years until on this night in 1999 as the club celebrated its sixtieth anniversary, its assets stood at just under $7,000,000.

Actually, it was worth far more because over the years almost three million dollars was withdrawn. Some members cashed in, some sold a portion of their portfolios and others deeded theirs to children or donated to charities.

The club's holdings, as reflected on the balance sheet at the anniversary dinner, bore silent testimony to the principle of investing over the long haul, and holding on to what you buy. Mutual held some of the securities for more than four decades. It held more than nineteen thousand shares of AFLAC insurance, bought at an average price of just fifty-two cents a share. In 1999, the stock was sold for close to fifty dollars a share. It bought General Electric decades before at $4.41. In 1999, after numerous splits, GE sold for $53 a share. It bought Intel at an average of $12.91. In 1999 it sold for over $133.

While the stock, once bought, usually stayed, it was not so with the members. Human mortality had taken its toll.

Only two of the original twelve members of the Mutual Investment Club were still alive. Tom O'Hara and Norm Hill.

Both had long since become millionaires. Both remained close friends.

Hill, who came along to the first meetings back at Fred Russell's Detroit house so he'd have an excuse to go out afterwards with his buddies and drink beer, flew to Nashville from his Grenada, Mississippi retirement home. He looked anything but a tycoon. The missing three fingers on his right hand testified to his background of hard, physical work as a tool and die man. They were sliced off in a machine accident in 1941, a year and a half after he and the others joined the club.

On this night in 1999, Hill made his way from table to table, warmly greeting old and new friends. When asked at one table to look back on the accomplishment of amassing so much wealth, Hill laughed and said he was still dumbfounded about how easy it had been. The initial ten dollar a month dues had gradually increased over the years but never to the point that Hill ever missed it. Like many investment club members, the experience was more social, he said, than selfish. He remembered his first reaction, back in 1985 or so, when it sunk in that he had become a millionaire through the club.

"At first, I didn't think it was mine," he said. "I never missed it. Honest to God, never. All those contributions over all those years, I never missed a dime. And when I saw how much it amounted to, my first reaction was, this can't be true. But it was. Saving regularly and reinvesting the interest works. Always. There's no secret. It really is that easy."

While O'Hara and Hill were the only surviving members in the year 2000 from the original bunch that gathered at Fred Russell's home back in 1940, the Mutual Investment Club still had a lot of old-timers.

Lew Rockwell, the Detroit attorney who drafted many of the original documents setting up NAIC and traveled frequently with O'Hara and George Nicholson in the early, formative years on NAIC business, joined the Mutual Club in 1943, when the dues had risen to twenty dollars a month. At the club's sixtieth anniversary dinner in Nashville, even at the age of eighty-one, Rockwell wanted everyone to know he still regularly did Stock Selection Guide studies.

In fact, everyone noticed Rockwell's enthusiasm. He excitedly touted his favorite stock, General Electric, and argued about the merits of his view with one of the newer members, Mark Robertson, who wasn't as keen on GE. Rockwell, whose sense of humor knows no bounds, made his points in that good-natured and kidding way old friends have when they get together.

Rockwell had also become a wealthy man. Like the others, he shrugged off the money. "That's not in the end the most important thing," he said. "It's the fabulous friendships you make, friendships that last your whole life. And the same principles that you learn about being wise with your money apply to every aspect of your life. It's a balanced, responsible approach to living. That's what you learn in an investment club. That, and not to take things too seriously. To understand that what may seem bad today will be better tomorrow. We also have complete honesty with each other. And nobody tries to do anything dishonest. It's a way of life that carries over in your daily living."

Ken Janke was also a member of the Mutual Investment Club. He joined shortly after Tom O'Hara hired him in 1960. Like most members, he formed several other clubs through the years. His wife Sally also formed clubs and continues to teach NAIC investing principles. The two beamed as they watched the Mutual members and their relatives file into the Nashville City Club.

"This is an amazing group," said Janke. "These people come from all over the country, from many different walks of life. And yet here, everyone's an equal. Everyone's a friend. Everyone's family."

The Janke's son, Ken Jr., was in attendance. He was a vice president with AFLAC, one of the stocks NAIC members have long favored and was in Nashville manning the AFLAC display at the NAIC Congress and Expo. The Janke's two daughters, Laura, an auditor at an accounting company, and Julie, an advertising executive, also embraced NAIC investing principles. So did Janke's late father, a former die maker with the Ford Motor Company.

It wasn't easy for Janke to convince his dad to invest in stocks. The elder Janke had seen what the 1929 stock crash did to investors and was worried when his son went to work for NAIC that he wouldn't have much of a future in a business dependent on stocks. Long after the son began turning handsome profits on investments, the father still balked. One day Ken Janke went to George Nicholson for advice, Nicholson suggested the son show the father some simple math.

"Doing a bit of mathematics homework, I was able to determine how many shares he would have to own of Detroit Edison so that his dividends would cover his electric bill," the man known as "Mr. NAIC" recalled. "We later did the same thing with Ford stock so the dividends plus his trade-in would allow him to buy a new automobile every three years."

Nicholson's advice worked and Janke's father became a happy investor. "When he retired, dad had more fun cashing dividend checks than he did receiving his monthly retirement and they usually increased on an annual basis. Those dividends exceeded his Social Security and retirement combined, as well."

Ken Janke wasn't the only one at the sixtieth anniversary meeting of the Mutual Investment Club with a lot of family memories tied up with the Club and NAIC.

Beth Nicholson Hamm, the daughter of George Nicholson sat a table near the side of the City Club dining area.

"This is my father's legacy," she said, emotion tugging at the edge of her voice as she looked around at the room full of smiling faces and old friends deep in conversation. "My father's goal was to help the average man be financially secure. In so doing, he believed that

that would make our nation secure. And a strong and secure America would make the world a better place. I think he must be looking down on us all tonight with a big grin on his face."

A couple of tables away from Beth Nicholson Hamm sat Tom and Eleanor O'Hara. They were surrounded by their daughters-in-law and their sons, Tom, Jr., a neurosurgeon from Ohio, and Robert, the NAIC Vice President of Business Development.

The NAIC theme of "Investing for a New Millennium" was on everyone's mind. Especially Tom O'Hara's.

It was a long way from the tough Depression-era streets of Southwest Detroit to the Chairman's office at NAIC. As a boy, looking up at the night stars from his backyard or on a campout with his teenage friends, O'Hara had often wondered what it would be like to live in the 21st century, when the years started with 20 instead of 19. In his wildest imagination he could not have pictured what his life would be like. Even in his eighty-fifth year, still healthy and vibrant, still with sparkling blue eyes that hinted at a fun-loving mischievousness, O'Hara daily thanked God for blessing him with family, friends and finances.

For besides those three F's of family, friends and finances, there was a fourth F.... faith. It was faith that drove Tom O'Hara most.

O'Hara's deep-seated faith in God and his determination to follow the Golden Rule was the driving force behind his personal and professional life. As a testimony to how important that faith was, Tom and Eleanor quietly donated more than one million dollars to establish a chair at a local Christian university, William Tyndale College. Another gift of half a million dollars went to their church to conduct meetings promoting Ecumenical support to missions.

The club meeting was amazingly short. The annual dinner meeting for friends and family was more of a social outing than a strict NAIC club business session, especially this meeting, celebrating sixty years of successful investing. After approving the minutes and reviewing the assets, sales and purchases, the members adjourned for desert and conversation.

After all, they were first of all friends.

Chapter Eight: **The Proof is in the Profits**

When all is said and done, no matter how nice the publications, how enthusiastic the computer chat room discussions, how admiring the press, when it comes to personal investments and a long-term plan for financial growth, it either works or it doesn't.

The profits paint the picture.

In the late 1990's, just about anyone who had anything invested in stocks or mutual funds did well. It was, in fact, the longest sustained bull market the economy had ever seen.

Then came 2000. The bull was blindsided and the bottom fell out. It started in the technology sector, ending wild speculation and sky-high stock prices that were based on hype and spin instead of the sound management and experience that NAIC preaches is what determines real value. The collapse of technology, led by the so-called Internet dot-com companies that turned into dot-bombs, was soon followed by a much deeper and more widespread market plunge.

The Dow Jones Industrial Index dropped 6.2 percent in 2000. Standard & Poor's were off 10.1 percent. The NASDAQ collapsed by more than fifty-two percent.

That was 2000.

It didn't get better during the first quarter of 2001.

The NASDAQ dropped another 25.5 percent from January through March of 2001, losing 630.26 points to close at 1,840.25. The Standard & Poor's 500 index lost 159.95 points, or 12.1 percent, to finish into a bear market for the first time since 1987. Wall Street generally says a bear market is when there has been a prolonged fall of twenty percent or more in a major index. The Dow, although less weighted to technology than the other major indexes, didn't suffer quite as badly, though it plummeted another 908.07 points, or 8.4 percent, to close the first quarter of 2001 at 9,878.78, on top of its 6.2 percent loss in year 2000.

With the new century off to such a dismal start, the acid test of the effort by Tom O'Hara and the three thousand plus NAIC volunteers to turn George Nicholson's dream into a great organization that truly produces wealthy investors was to simply look at the accounts of the members. If they lost as much or more than everybody else, well, so much for their claims of better investing the NAIC way and so much for the credibility of the organization. On the other hand, if members were more successful than comparable sectors of the nation's investing public, then the principles that guided NAIC would be vindicated through perhaps the most volatile and strenuous economic conditions ever encountered during the group's half-century existence.

The statistics are pretty stunning.

Their numbers are noticeably better.

Their bottom-line is better.

Their performance proves the principles.

The records show that amateur investors following NAIC principles have consistently earned rates of income on their investments that regularly exceed that of the popular averages like the Dow and Standard & Poor's 500 Index.

Probably the best way to measure the performance of NAIC investors is to look at the NAIC Top 100 Index. Each year, all of NAIC's member clubs are asked to send a copy of their portfolio to the organization's headquarters in Madison Heights. "We believe that the NAIC Top 100 is a representative benchmark of the aggregate results achieved by NAIC investors," reads the preface to the list published on the *Better Investing* magazine Web site (www.better-investing.com). The NAIC Top 100 annualized total return for the five years ending on February 28, 2001 was 19.1 percent, versus 15.9 percent for the S&P 500 and the Dow.

That's impressive.

E. Brooke Harrington is an Assistant Professor of Sociology and Public Policy at Harvard University. As part of her PhD research in 1998, she sent out a two-part survey to three thousand randomly selected NAIC clubs to gather information on individual members, their demographic characteristics and investment practices. Her study was the most comprehensive ever undertaken on the organization, providing an extremely rich data set that, unlike previous research, allowed her to link individual behavior to group outcomes. In other words, by carefully analyzing the responses, she could actually test how following the NAIC investment principles actually affected club performance.

In all, 1,236 clubs participated in her survey, about forty-one percent of the three thousand surveys sent out. Of them, ninety, or just over seven percent, were all-men clubs; 667 (fifty-four percent) were all-women's clubs and 467 (thirty-eight percent) were mixed clubs.

Here are highlights of what she found:

The average age of an NAIC club was 4.33 years. The vast majority of clubs, eighty percent, are under five years old. The clubs meet an average of eleven times a year, include about sixteen members with an average age of fifty and maintain an average portfolio of $41,000, made up of nine stocks. The individual club members have an income of $50,000 to $75,000. Most are college educated, over seventy-six percent own a computer and most use it to track investments, surf the Internet for research, or find potential investments. Club members spend about four hours a month on club-related work and usually attend at least one seminar or NAIC training event each year.

The research provided extremely detailed profiles of the typical NAIC member. Eighty percent said they invested primarily for retirement. The average member has, besides his club holdings, a personal investment portfolio worth $100,000, which sixty-two percent directly manage themselves. Most did their own research in buying a stock. About thirty-five percent said they relied on a broker for most of their decisions.

Harrington took all this data, and much more, and came up with five predictors of investment club performance. They are:

- Club Age – Up to about five years of age, every additional month a club is in operation increased performance by twenty three percent. After five years, experience seems to be maximized and additional time has negligible effect.
- Cash holdings – For every percentage point of a club's portfolio that remained uninvested, performance decreased by seventeen percent.
- Time as a member – The greater the ratio of new members to total membership in the club, the worse the club will do.
- Member motivation – the more interested members are in investment instead of socialization, the better the club will do.
- Average household income of club members – The lower the average income of club members, the better the club performs.

Taking all this data into consideration, what did Harrington discover? In short: following the principles…works.

The proof is indeed in the profits.

"Employing NAIC principles leads to increased financial returns," she wrote. Because the survey was in such depth, she was able to compare clubs that followed the guidelines and those that didn't. "Clubs that don't follow these guidelines don't do as well...The evidence finds that investment clubs earn higher financial returns to the extent that they follow NAIC methods."

The key, as O'Hara and Nicholson insisted all along, is education, investing experience, and faith in the patient, persistent and profitable principles espoused by NAIC.

On a bright sunny April day in 2001, O'Hara, tanned and refreshed after spending much of the winter with Eleanor in his Florida retirement home, reflected on a half-century of investment lessons. Still active with NAIC, he was contemplating moving back to Michigan for the summer, before the hot weather engulfed the Sunshine State. It would be a busy year, planning for the NAIC fiftieth anniversary Congress, to be held that fall in Detroit. Even into his eighth decade, his blue eyes still twinkled at the thought of being together with so many friends, both old and new, many of whom owed their financial security to what they had been taught by the organization O'Hara founded. And then there was Christmas to anticipate with two new grandchildren expected, adding to the two he and Eleanor already had.

The O'Haras were enjoying a good life. Besides a comfortable Florida winter home and a luxurious condominium on the Detroit River that overlooks the downtown Detroit skyline, they also owned a summer place in Northern Michigan. A millionaire several times over because of his investment practices, O'Hara was also mused to find himself a celebrity, thanks to a popular print ad by the AFLAC insurance company that depicted him holding the company's trademark white duck on the floor of the New York Stock Exchange. AFLAC was one of the most held stocks by NAIC members and O'Hara perfectly symbolized the company's appreciation of the small, faithful investor.

Yet, beneath the affluence and notoriety and the deep respect bestowed on him by the investment community, Tom O'Hara was still the same as the Depression-era teenager from southwest Detroit who determined decades before not to end up like those haunted men who once stood on street corners selling apples and pencils through no fault of their own. He had seen the worst economic times the world has ever encountered. He had also seen the best. Between the extremes came the secret to success.

He had watched the market turbulence of 2000 and 2001, of course, spending, as was his daily habit over decades, an hour or so a day reading the financial pages and market reports. He did so calmly, as a student — passionately interested, but never apprehensive, for there were no deep concerns about the inherent soundness of the nation's economic system. Three times O'Hara has seen market plunges. And three times… in the thirties, the sixties and seventies… he has seen bear market conditions turn bullish. Three times he had seen how NAIC principles performed flawlessly. That kind of perspective gives a man a steadiness, an optimism.

He remembered back in the sixties when the portfolio of the Mutual Investment Club reached a net worth of a half million dollars. It was a heady time, soon dashed when the market plunged. Members helplessly watched as bear conditions cut the value of their holdings to $280,000. However, they never wavered, renewing their commitment to stay the course, to follow the principles, pick the best companies and keep investing no matter what the market conditions. That bear market basically got worse and worse. For eighteen years the market declined or stagnated. But when it finally turned bull again in the eighties, the mutual holdings dramatically rose, appreciating in value to $1.4 million.

No, the market gyrations of early 2001 were to be expected. O'Hara told the many who asked. Just as the continued growth in value of market investments could be expected, too, if only those investments were carefully made… the NAIC way. It has never been more important to do so, with a large percentage of the population now being blessed with retirement fund options. In O'Hara's thinking, the incentive these options bring to invest regularly and wisely, combined with personal investing opportunities, make doing things right doubly important. Financial independence hangs in the balance.

Truly, O'Hara's has been a journey of a lifetime. A journey born in the midst of a world war, spread through station-wagon whistle-stop visits across the land, and brought to full maturity with the revolution in communications and information as the century turned. It has been a journey his old friend George Nicholson encouraged him to take, one that indeed has mass-produced capitalists.

Yet for all the lives touched and helped along the way, O'Hara sees capitalism's finest hour as yet to come. "This great nation has set the goal of freedom for every person. Economic freedom is a basic part of that goal. Helping individuals learn how to use the opportunity in that freedom to build a better future for themselves and their loved ones is the reason for all our work.

"It's not a job. It's a crusade. Leadership changes, but the cause continues."

NAIC Background and Appendices

Headquarters:
711 W. 13 Mile Road
Madison Heights, MI 48071
877/275-6242
248/583-4880 FAX
Web site: www.better-investing.org

Established:
October 1951 by four investment clubs in Detroit, Michigan.

Founding Members:
George A. Nicholson, Fredrick C. Russell and Thomas E. O'Hara

Purpose:
NAIC is a non-profit, tax exempt organization whose membership consists of investment clubs and individual investors. NAIC was founded in 1951 with a mission to provide a program of sound investment information, education and support that helps create successful, lifetime investors. NAIC's programs, services and products are designed to help individuals of all knowledge levels to become successful, long-term investors. NAIC members' investment portfolios have consistently outperformed market averages. NAIC has provided investment education to more than five million individuals and is a charter member of the World Federation of Investors, providing investment education in over seventeen countries worldwide.

151

Trustees
Thomas E. O'Hara – Chairman
Kenneth S. Janke, Sr. – President and CEO
Lewis A. Rockwell – Secretary
Robert W. Hague – Treasurer
Warren B. Alexander, Donald E. Danko, Lorrie Gustin, Elizabeth N. Hamm, Richard A. Holthaus, Kenneth R. Lightcap, Leroy F. Mumford, Peggy L. Schmeltz, Ralph L. Seger, Jr., Robert L. Wynn

Board of Advisors
James L. Agee
Helen J. McLane

National Investors Association Board of Directors
Shirley Knudsen, Chairman
Chris Curtis, President
Gary V. Ball, Vice President
Elizabeth A. Sinnock, Vice President
Jo Ann Linck, Secretary
Robert V. Blailock, Treasurer

Directors: William P. Agster, Stephen W. Beer, Emma Dimpfel, Mary Lyn Fledderman, Evonne A. Hurst, Donna Jones, Hugh McManus, Mimi Rauschelbach, Lary Reno, Quentin Sampson, Billy M. Williams, Saundra Wall Williams, Pat Wood

Associate Directors: Linda Blay, Patrick Connell, Jennifer Evans, Carol Haverty, Robert S. Kovach, Monica Noel, Ingeborg Steinke, Anne Uno

Directors Emeriti: Edward Bierman, Cynthia P. Charles, Leland B. Finkbeiner, Richard G. Horak, John M. Paterson, Robert L. Showalter, Robert L. Tice, Lennart Width

Computer Group Board of Directors
Werner H. Wahl, Chairman
Philip J. Keating, CFA Honorary Chairman
Pamela Wright, President
Bob Adams, Vice President
Joe N. Craig, Ph.D, Vice President
Nancy Crays, Ph.D, Vice President
Douglas Gerlach, Secretary
Bob Schaelchlin, Treasurer
Sandra F. Barlow
Herbert K. Barnett
Chris Collins
Mary Ann Davis
Cy Lynch
Leslie Wilkinson
Bart Womack

Assistant Directors
Michael Bacsa
Kathy Boettcher
Marilee Catalano
Nancy DeGraff
Diane Graese
Kenneth A. Halwas
Pat McVey-Ritsick
Ken J. Morris
Janet Rannenberg
Calvin Richards
David Roche
Louise Sechler
Saul Seinberg
Bill Thomas
Semour Zeenkov

NAIC Philosophy and Membership

Investment Philosophy

NAIC encourages its members to follow four investing principles:

- Invest a set amount regularly, usually once a month, regardless of market conditions.
- Reinvest all dividends and capital gains.
- Buy growth stocks – companies whose sales are increasing at a rate faster than industry in general and with the potential of doubling in value in the next five years
- Diversify your portfolio – invest in different industries and different size companies.

Membership

As of June 2001, NAIC's membership is comprised of the following:

- NAIC's membership – individual and investment club members
- Investment clubs
- Individuals
- Computer Group
- Corporate Advisors and Supporters

Approximately 2,500 NAIC members volunteer to serve the 116 NAIC Regional Chapters, which conduct investing seminars, workshops, computer events and Investor Fairs® across the country throughout the year.

National Association of Investors Corporation (NAIC) Fact Sheet

- 54% are female and 46% are male
- Median age of NAIC members is 54 years
- Average investment club age is 4 years

Value of Equity Investments
Average NAIC member personal portfolio value:
$353,500 each

Average NAIC investment club portfolio value:
$106,000

Total portfolio value of all NAIC members:
$197 BILLION

Total new money invested monthly by NAIC members:
$247 MILLION

Investment Habits of NAIC Members (2000 Survey)
Average NAIC member's annual return on investments:
17.9%

Average amount that NAIC investment clubs invest each month:
$928

Average length of time that an NAIC member holds a stock:
6 years

NAIC's Four Easy Investment Principles

NAIC principles for investing are basic and have been producing financial success for individuals and investment clubs for over 45 years.

The four basic principles are:

1. Invest regular sums of money once a month in common stock. This helps you obtain a lower average cost on your investments.

2. Reinvest all earnings, dividends and capital gains. Your money grows faster if earnings are reinvested. This way, compounding of your money is at work for you.

3. Buy growth stocks—companies whose sales and earnings are consistently increasing at a rate faster than the industry in general. They should have good prospects for continued growth or, in other words, they should be stronger, larger companies five years from now.

4. Invest in different industries. Diversification helps spread both risk and opportunity.

Mutual Fund Investing
NAIC has an Investment Manual especially for mutual fund investors and forms to test the potential of funds you are interested in.

NAIC Membership

As an individual investor or as a member of an investment club, NAIC's investment programs are designed to help you build and accumulate wealth. They are not get-rich-quick programs. For a few years you accumulate experience and skill. Then as your skill and funds grow, your profits are likely to become larger.

Getting started is important. The sooner you start, the sooner you will have a year's experience and accumulation behind you, and the sooner you will be able to say, "I'm a lot better off now than I was five years ago!"

NAIC Membership Categories

NAIC offers two ways to build your investment know-how and future wealth — as an investment club member or as an individual member.

Investment Club Membership

It is not necessary to have investment knowledge or sizeable funds to start an investment club. Usually a small group of people — often ten to twenty — join together to learn NAIC's investment principles and how to enact them. Most groups meet once a month, contribute $20 to $50, review studies of stocks presented by members, and select one or more stocks in which to invest. By the end of the year, they will have studied and bought several stocks, and expanded their knowledge of a number of individual companies, and the stock market in general.

Individual Membership

An individual may wish to learn about investing on his/her own while investing small sums regularly over a period of time. Don't underestimate the potential for the long-term growth of your money. Remember, your knowledge will grow as the amount of money you invest grows. NAIC members have built a record of outstanding investment performance including many who consistently outperform the Standard & Poor's 500 Index. You can become a member simply by sending your request to NAIC with a check for your first year dues

Computer Group Membership
NAIC's Computer Group is a special interest group for individuals and investment clubs interested in enhancing their investing skills through the use of computer aids. The NAIC Computer Group offers its members a host of services and activities to help them become more effective and successful long-term investors.

NAIC Computer Group – Includes ten issues of *BITS*, plus a special *BITS* Super Database, discounts on NAIC software and computer events, online services and activities through the NAIC Forum.

These opportunities are spelled out for you on the web site and in NAIC's new Membership Guide, which includes information on membership, supplies, and services available to you through NAIC, 711 W. 13 Mile Road, Madison Heights, MI 48071

Youth Membership
Recent surveys have shown that high school seniors are graduating with little or no knowledge about personal finance and investing. No matter which career a student enters, he or she will be an investor. Many people wait until they are in their middle years of life before they even start to think about learning the basics of personal finance and investing. In 1996, NAIC started a program geared toward helping a younger generation of potential investors learn about the basics of personal finance and investing. The first offering was a home-study course written for teens, entitled *Investing for Life*. In early 2000, NAIC authored its first book to be distributed in America's high schools, *Investing in Your Future* (complete with interactive CD-ROM). Today, youngsters can join as NAIC Youth Members, and receive an informative newsletter written for them. NAIC has found that four basic principles and several investment tools can offer beginners (especially young students) some real life lessons that will provide a solid foundation for lifetime learning. In

158

addition, the formation of investment clubs by teachers and students have been shown to offer "hands-on" activities that provide the opportunities for critical thinking skills and leadership skills.

Membership Benefits

NAIC Official Guide – This Guide for learn-by-doing investing contains NAIC's full stock study program. The Guide can help you improve your personal investment performance and add value to your investment club.

Better Investing – A monthly magazine for the individual investor providing current investment information, market news and many other wealth-building and investment education features.

NAIC's Young Money Matters Newsletter – An investment education newsletter for youths featuring real-life stories of young investor experiences, educational exercises and fun games to teach youths about money concepts, saving and investing.

Investor's Information Sheets – These stock fact sheets are reports that provide financial information of interest to the long-term investor. They are presented in the same format as the NAIC Stock Selection Guide with more than one hundred available, and free to members.

Local NAIC Chapter support & seminars – Located throughout the United States, Chapters are made up of volunteer NAIC members who help individuals and clubs.

National Congress and Expo – NAIC's premier gathering of long-term investors throughout the nation, featuring a three-day conference and one of the largest displays of investment information and ideas in the world. The NAIC Congress includes general sessions, investment seminars, workshops, corporate roundtable discussions, more than 150 corporate exhibits and presentations, featured nationally known speakers, tours, social events and much more. All this surrounded by the fun and excitement of the selected Expo city.

CompuFest – NAIC's annual gathering of individual investors from around the nation who are interested in learning how to use a computer to invest the NAIC way. Seminars and computer labs are offered for investors of all age levels, including young investors. Windows and Macintosh programs are featured, as well as seminars and one-on-one instruction labs on all NAIC stock study accounting software. Corporate and vendor exhibits, discussion areas and presentations offer additional investing information.

InvestFest – An NAIC national event that provides the same focus on NAIC's methods of successful investing for investors in a specific region of the United States. Included are nationally known speakers, informative seminars, corporate presentations, computer demonstrations and a "hands-on learning" lab area.

For any information dial toll-free 877-275-6242.

Appendix A

The National Association of Investors Corporation, originally named The National Association of Investment Clubs, was formed on August 28, 1961 when the founding Trustees met at the Engineering Society of Detroit in the Rackham Building and signed the Trust Agreement. The founding Trustees and the current Trustees, as well as all the officers in all of the divisions of NAIC are volunteers and have given outstanding and inspirational leadership to NAIC throughout its fifty years of service to millions of investors.

Most rewarding to all of them has been the quality and effectiveness of NAIC's investment principles and the teaching skill of its volunteers which have made millions of NAIC members some of the most successful investors in the nation.

NAIC is under the management and direction of its Board of Trustees. The first Board consisted of individuals who were most interested in getting the group started. New Trustees are chosen by the existing Trustees. To facilitate its operation, it has formed a number of divisions. The largest and oldest division is the National Investors Association (NIA). This group is managed by Directors, chosen annually by members, and confirmed by the Board of Trustees. This division conducts NAIC's annual national Congress and develops and supervises NAIC's regional Chapters. These Chapters carry NAIC's educational programs directly to members in their hometowns. Currently there are 116 Chapters serving most major population centers in the United States.

Following are the Boards of Trustees that have helped to build the organization.

NAIC TRUSTEES

August 28, 1951

Thomas E. O'Hara, Chairman
Robert L. Pryor, Secretary
Robert A. Burger, Treasurer
F. Russell Amerman
Arthur F. Baske
Richard Dibner
Frederick N. McOmber
Frederick C. Russell
Vernon L. Schiller

February 1956

Thomas E. O'Hara, Chairman
Robert L. Pryor, Secretary
Robert A. Burger, Treasurer
Richard Dibner (Resigned, July)
Frederick N. McOmber
Paul R. Miller (Joined, December)
Lewis A. Rockwell
Frederick C. Russell
Vernon L. Schiller

May 1964

Thomas E. O'Hara, Chairman
Robert L. Pryor, Secretary
Robert A. Burger, Treasurer
Frederick N. McOmber
Paul R. Miller
Lewis A. Rockwell
Frederick C. Russell
  (Deceased, July 1965)
Vernon L. Schiller
Ralph L. Seger, Jr.

June 1969

Thomas E. O'Hara, Chairman
Robert L. Pryor, Secretary
Robert A. Burger, Treasurer
Warren B. Alexander
Helen J. McLane
Frederick N. McOmber
Paul R. Miller
Lewis A. Rockwell
Vernon L. Schiller
Ralph L. Seger, Jr.

October 1972

Thomas E. O'Hara, Chairman
Robert L. Pryor, Secretary
Robert A. Burger, Treasurer
Warren B. Alexander
Helen J. McLane
  (Resigned, October 1972)
Frederick N. McOmber
  (Resigned, April 1974)
Paul R. Miller
  (Deceased, April 1975)
Lewis A. Rockwell
Vernon L. Schiller
Ralph L. Seger, Jr.

June 1977

Thomas E. O'Hara, Chairman
Robert L. Pryor, Secretary
Robert A. Burger, Treasurer
Warren B. Alexander
Leroy F. Mumford
Lewis A. Rockwell
Vernon L. Schiller
Ralph L. Seger, Jr.

May 1979

Thomas E. O'Hara, Chairman
Robert L. Pryor, Secretary
Robert A. Burger, Treasurer
Warren B. Alexander
Lorrie Gustin
Kenneth S. Janke
Leroy F. Mumford
Lewis A. Rockwell
Vernon L. Schiller
  (Resigned, July 1981)
Ralph L. Seger, Jr.

September 1981

Thomas E. O'Hara, Chairman
Kenneth S. Janke,
  President & CEO
Robert L. Pryor, Secretary
Robert A. Burger, Treasurer
Warren B. Alexander
Donald E. Danko
Lorrie Gustin
Robert W. Hague
Leroy F. Mumford

Lewis A. Rockwell
Ralph L. Seger, Jr.

November 1982

Thomas E. O'Hara, Chairman
Kenneth S. Janke,
  President & CEO
Robert L. Pryor, Secretary
Robert A. Burger, Treasurer
Warren B. Alexander
Donald E. Danko
Lorrie Gustin
Robert W. Hague
Kenneth R. Lightcap
Leroy F. Mumford
Lewis A. Rockwell
Ralph L. Seger, Jr.

June 1987

Thomas E. O'Hara, Chairman
Kenneth S. Janke,
  President & CEO
Lewis A. Rockwell, Secretary
Robert A. Burger, Treasurer
Warren B. Alexander
Donald E. Danko
Lorrie Gustin
Robert W. Hague
Richard A. Holthaus
Kenneth R. Lightcap
Leroy F. Mumford
Robert L. Pryor
Ralph L. Seger, Jr.

163

June 1993

Thomas E. O'Hara, Chairman
Kenneth S. Janke,
  President & CEO
Lewis A. Rockwell, Secretary
Robert A. Burger, Treasurer
  (Deceased, August 1993)
Warren B. Alexander
Donald E. Danko
Lorrie Gustin
Robert W. Hague
Richard A. Holthaus
Kenneth R. Lightcap
Leroy F. Mumford
Robert L. Pryor
Ralph L. Seger, Jr.
Sharon L. Vuinovich

August 1993

Thomas E. O'Hara, Chairman
Kenneth S. Janke,
  President & CEO
Lewis A. Rockwell, Secretary
Robert W. Hague, Treasurer
Warren B. Alexander
Donald E. Danko
Lorrie Gustin
Richard A. Holthaus
Kenneth R. Lightcap
Leroy F. Mumford
Robert L. Pryor
Ralph L. Seger, Jr.
Sharon L. Vuinovich

October 1995

Thomas E. O'Hara, Chairman
Kenneth S. Janke,
  President & CEO
Lewis A. Rockwell, Secretary
Robert W. Hague, Treasurer
Warren B. Alexander
Donald E. Danko
Lorrie Gustin
Richard A. Holthaus
Kenneth R. Lightcap
Leroy F. Mumford
Robert L. Pryor (Deceased,
October 1995)
Peggy L. Schmeltz
Ralph L. Seger, Jr.
Sharon L. Vuinovich

January 1996

Thomas E. O'Hara, Chairman
Kenneth S. Janke,
  President & CEO
Lewis A. Rockwell, Secretary
Robert W. Hague, Treasurer
Warren B. Alexander
Donald E. Danko
Lorrie Gustin
Elizabeth N. Hamm
Richard A. Holthaus
Kenneth R. Lightcap
Leroy F. Mumford
Peggy L. Schmeltz
Ralph L. Seger, Jr.
Sharon L. Vuinovich
  (Resigned, September 1998)

February 1999 To Current

Thomas E. O'Hara, Chairman
Kenneth S. Janke, President & CEO
Lewis A. Rockwell, Secretary
Robert W. Hague, Treasurer
Warren B. Alexander
Donald E. Danko
Lorrie Gustin
Elizabeth N. Hamm
Richard A. Holthaus
Kenneth R. Lightcap
Leroy F. Mumford
Peggy L. Schmeltz
Ralph L. Seger, Jr.
Robert L. Wynn, II

Following are the Boards of Directors that have brought NAIC's investment principles and stock selection procedures to individuals across the country.

First National Board,

October 1951

Wagar A. Glas, Chairman
Lewis A. Rockwell, President
Haig Avedisian, Vice President
Robert Stoetzer, Vice President
Elizabeth Kaufmann, Secretary
James Youd, Treasurer
John F. Anderson
Richard Dibner
Benjamin Dickinson

James Fancher
James H. Hood, Jr.
  (Joined, June 1952)
Edgar Hornik
Lyndon Kaufmann
Paul R. Miller (Joined, July 1952)
George Woods

November 1952

Wagar A. Glas, Chairman
Lewis A. Rockwell, President
Elizabeth Kaufmann, Secretary
Benjamin Dickinson, Treasurer
Haig Avedisian
Norman E. Hill
James H. Hood, Jr.
Edgar Hornik
James R. S. Millar
Paul R. Miller
William K. Sanford

December 1953

Wagar A. Glas, Chairman
Lewis A. Rockwell, President
Elizabeth Kaufmann, Secretary
Benjamin Dickinson, Treasurer
Norman E. Hill
Calvin Hobart
James H. Hood, Jr.
Leo H. Jacobson
James R. S. Millar
Paul R. Miller
William K. Sanford
George Squire
Helen Stege

October 1954

Wagar A. Glas, Chairman
Helen Stege, President
Donald T. Mathis, Secretary
Benjamin Dickinson, Treasurer
Alex Carroll
Chester Drake
Leland B. Finkbeiner
Robert E. Fletcher
William Minot Thomas
William J. Thompson
Charles S. Urquhart

October 1955

Wagar A. Glas, Chairman
Helen Stege, President
Grace Davidson, Secretary
James R. S. Millar, Treasurer
Robert F. Brang
Alex Carroll
Robert E. Davis
Chester Drake
Leland B. Finkbeiner
Robert E. Fletcher
Leo H. Jacobson
James E. Kirkendall
William T. Mabee
Donald T. Mathis
Paul R. Miller
William Minot Thomas
(Deceased, August 1956)
William J. Thompson
Charles S. Urquhart

November 1956

Wagar A. Glas, Chairman
Helen Stege, President
Grace Davidson, Secretary
James R. S. Millar, Treasurer
Richard Boynton
Robert E. Brang
Pierre L. Bretay
Alex Carroll
Francis J. Coyne
Robert E. Davis
Leland B. Finkbeiner
Robert E. Fletcher
Leo H. Jacobson
Alec S. Lubnik
William T. Mabee
Donald T. Mathis
Paul R. Miller
Carl E. Swartz
William J. Thompson
Charles S. Urquhart
Rollin P. Woodward

November 1957

Wagar A. Glas, Chairman
Leland B. Finkbeiner, President
Jean M. Alfsen, Secretary
James R. S. Millar, Treasurer
Richard Boynton
Pierre L. Bretay
Alex Carroll
Francis J. Coyne
Robert E. Fletcher
John Hedlesky
Edwin W. Husen

Alec J. Lubnik
William T. Mabee
John Reissenweber
Ralph L. Seger, Jr.
Helen Stege
Carl W. Swartz
Charles S. Urquhart
Rollin P. Woodward

November 1958

Wagar A. Glas, Chairman
William T. Mabee, President
Ralph L. Seger, Jr.,
  First Vice President
Robert L. Showalter,
  Second Vice President
Helen J. McLane,
  Third Vice President
Jean M. Alfsen, Secretary
James R. S. Millar, Treasurer
Leland B. Finkbeiner
Robert E. Fletcher
John Hockman
Edwin W. Husen
Alec S. Lubnik
T. Lewis Moore
John Reissenweber
Helen Stege
Edgar D. Werner
Rollin P. Woodward

October 1959

Wagar A. Glas, Chairman
William T. Mabee, President
Ralph L. Seger, Jr.,
  First Vice President
Robert L. Showalter,
  Second Vice President
Helen J. McLane,
  Third Vice President
Rollin P. Woodward, Secretary
James R. S. Millar, Treasurer
James L. Agee
Jean M. Alfsen
Thomas J. Auchter
Marvin T. Deane
Winona Devlin (Resigned,
September 1960)
Leland B. Finkbeiner
Robert E. Fletcher
Edwin W. Husen
Alec S. Lubnik

October 1960

Wagar A. Glas, Chairman
Ralph L. Seger, Jr., President
Robert L. Showalter,
  First Vice President
Helen J. McLane,
  Second Vice President
Robert E. Fletcher,
  Third Vice President
Rollin P. Woodward, Secretary
James R.S. Millar, Treasurer
  (Resigned, January 1961)

Alec S. Lubnik, Treasurer
  (Appointed, January 1961)
James L. Agee
Jean M. Alfsen
Thomas J. Auchter
Marvin T. Deane
Leland B. Finkbeiner
Joseph L. Herlihy
Edwin W. Husen
William T. Mabee
Joseph J. Miller, Jr.
T. Lewis Moore
Lewis Nachman
B. Evans Roth
Carl E. Swartz
Edgar D. Werner

October 1961

Wagar A. Glas, Chairman
Ralph L. Seger, Jr., President
Robert L. Showalter,
  First Vice President
B. Evans Roth,
  Second Vice President
Lewis Moore,
  Third Vice President
Rollin P. Woodward, Secretary
Alec S. Lubnik, Treasurer
James L. Agee
Warren B. Alexander
Jean M. Alfsen
Marvin T. Deane
Marion W. Dickey
Leland B. Finkbeiner
Robert E. Fletcher

James F. Fox
Joseph L. Herlihy
William T. Mabee
  (Resigned, July 1962)
Evan D. MacLeod
Helen J. McLane
James R. S. Millar
Joseph J. Miller, Jr.
Lewis Nachman
Carl E. Swartz
Edgar D. Werner

October 1962

Wagar A. Glas, Chairman
Ralph L. Seger, Jr., President
Warren B. Alexander,
  Vice President
James F, Fox, Vice President
T. Lewis Moore, Vice President
Evan D. MacLeod, Secretary
Alec S. Lubnik, Treasurer
James L. Agee
Jean M. Alfsen
Marvin T. Deane
Marion W. Dickey
George J. Eberhardt
Leland B. Finkbeiner
Robert E. Fletcher
Carl C. Hall
Wilbur T. Hardison
Joseph L. Herlihy
Helen J. McLane
James R. S. Millar
Joseph L. Miller, Jr.
Leroy F. Mumford

Lewis Nachman
B. Evans Roth
Robert L. Showalter
Edgar D. Werner

October 1963

Wagar A. Glas, Chairman
Warren B. Alexander, President
James L. Agee, Vice President
James F. Fox, Vice President
Leroy F. Mumford, Vice President
Robert E. Fletcher, Secretary
Alec S. Lubnik, Treasurer
Paul J. Brexnen
  Appointed, March 1964
Marvin T. Deane
Alvin O. Diamond
  (Appointed, December 1963)
Marion W. Dickey
George J. Eberhardt
Leland B. Finkbeiner
Carl C. Hall
  (Resigned, December 1963)
William T. Hardison
  (Appointed, March 1964)
Joseph L. Herlihy
Charles Mackie
Evan D. MacLeod
Helen J. McLane
Ruth C. McPhetridge
James R. S. Millar
T. Lewis Moore
  (Resigned, December 1963)
Ralph L. Seger, Jr.
Robert L. Showalter

Witold T. Sikorski
  (Appointed, December 1963)
Edgar D. Werner

November 1964

Wagar A. Glas, Chairman
Warren B. Alexander, President
James L. Agee, Vice President
Leroy F. Mumford, Vice President
Robert E. Fletcher, Secretary
Alec S. Lubnik Treasurer
Elaine M. Benson
Marvin T. Deane
Alvin O. Diamond
Marion W. Dickey
George J. Eberhardt
James F. Fox
Charles Mackie
Helen J. McLane
Ruth C. McPhedridge
James R. S. Millar
James P. Montgomery
Ralph L. Seger, Jr.
Robert L. Showalter
Edgar D. Werner

October 1965

Wagar A. Glas, Chairman
Warren B. Alexander, President
James L. Agee, Vice Presdent
Marion W. Dickey, Vice President
James F. Fox, Vice President
Leroy F. Mumford, Vice President
Witold T. Sikorski, Vice President
Robert E. Fletcher, Secretary

169

Alec S. Lubnik, Treasurer
Elaine M. Benson
Paul J. Breznen
Alvin O. Diamond
George J. Eberhardt
Leland B. Finkbeiner
Helen J. McLane
Ruth C. McPhedridge
James R. S. Millar
Pames P. Montgomery
Jean M. Palacz
Ralph L. Seger, Jr.
Robert L. Showalter
Edgar D. Werner

November 1966

Wagar A. Glas, Chairman
Warren B. Alexander, President
James L. Agee, Vice President
Marion W. Dickey, Vice President
James F. Fox, Vice President
Leroy F. Mumford, Vice President
Robert E. Fletcher, Secretary
Alec S. Lubnik, Treasurer
Elaine M. Benson
Paul J. Breznen
Alvin O. Diamond
Donald M. Douglas
George J. Eberhardt
Leland B. Finkbeiner
Lorrie Gustin
Helen J. McLane
Ruth C. McPhetridge
James R. S. Millar
Jean M. Palacz
Leonard I. Reiser

Ralph L. Seger, Jr.
Robert L. Showlater
Witold T. Sikorski
Fern L. Wilson

October 1967

Wagar A. Glas, Chairman
Warren B. Alexander, President
Marion W. Dickey, Vice President
Donald M. Douglas,
  Vice President
Helen J. McLane, Vice President
Leroy F. Mumford, Vice President
Robert E. Fletcher, Secretary
Alec S. Lubnik, Treasurer
James L. Agee
Elaine M. Benson
Paul J. Breznen
Cynthia P. Charles
James L. Cregg
Alvin O. Diamond
George J. Eberhardt
Leland B. Finkbeiner
James F. Fox
Lorrie Gustin
Keith A. Leibbrand
William P. McGregor
Ruth C. McPhetridge
James R. S. Millar
Edward H. Mueller
Jean M. Palacz
Leonard I. Reiser
Witold T. Sikorski
Marianne G. Vethacke
Fern L. Wilson

October 1968

Wagar A. Glas, Chairman
Warren B. Alexander, President
Donald M. Douglas,
  Vice President
Helen J. McLane, Vice President
Leroy F. Mumford, Vice President
Robert L. Showalter,
  Vice President
Fern L. Wilson, Vice President
Robert E. Fletcher, Secretary
Alec S. Lubnik, Treasurer
James L. Agee
Elaine M. Benson
Paul J. Breznen
Duane S. Carr
Cynthia P. Charles
James L. Cregg
Alvin O. Diamond
Marion W. Dickey
Leland B. Finkbeiner
James F. Fox
  (Deceased, March 1969)
Lorrie Gustin
Keith A. Leibbrand
William P. McGregor
Ruth C. McPhetridge
James R. S. Millar
Edward H. Mueller
Jean M. Palacz
Leonard I. Reiser
Carolyn L. Schwartz
Witold T. Sikorski
Marianne G. Vethacke
Lee A. Wilbur

October 1969

Warren B. Alexander, Chairman
James L. Agee, President
Marion W. Dickey, Vice President
Leroy F. Mumford, Vice President
Leonard I. Reiser, Vice President
Robert L. Showalter,
  Vice President
Witold T. Sikorski, Vice President
Lorrie Gustin, Secretary
Alec S. Lubnik, Treasurer
James L. Cregg, Assistant
  Treasurer
Jean M. Alfsen
Elaine M. Benson
Paul J. Breznen
Duane S. Carr
Cynthia P. Charles
Leland B. Finkbeiner
Robert E. Fletcher
Keith A. Leibbrand
William P. McGregor
Ruth C. McPhetridge
James R. S. Millar
Edward H. Mueller
Norman A. Nystrom
Jean M. Palacz
Darvin E. Schroeder
Carolyn L. Schwartz
Marianne G. Vethacke
Lee A. Wilbur
Fern L. Wilson

171

October 1970

Warren B. Alexander, Chairman
James L. Agee, President
Ruth C. McPhetridge,
  Vice President
Leroy F. Mumford, Vice President
Leonard I. Reiser, Vice President
Lorrie Gustin, Secretary
Alec S. Lubnik, Treasurer
Witold T. Sikorski,
  Assistant Treasurer
Duane S. Carr
Cynthia P. Charles
Marion W. Dickey
Leland B. Finkbeiner
Robert E. Fletcher
Keith A. Leibbrand
John Loomer
William P. McGregor
James R. S. Millar
Edward H. Mueller
Norman A. Nystrom
Jean M. Palacz
Darvin E. Schroeder
Robert L. Showalter
Louis Toenjes
Marianne G. Vethacke
Lee A. Wilbur
Fern L. Wilson

October 1971

Warren B. Alexander, Chairman
James L. Agee, President
Ruth C. McPhetridge,
  Vice President

Leonard I. Reiser, Vice President
Darvin E. Schroeder,
  Vice President
Keith A. Leibbrand, Secretary
Alec S. Lubnik, Treasurer
Witold T. Sikorski,
  Assistant Secretary
Jean M. Alfsen
Duane S. Carr
Cynthia P. Charles
David M. Crowley
Marion W. Dickey
Leland B. Finkbeiner
Robert E. Fletcher
Lorrie Gustin
Leon E. Hoffer
John Loomer
William P. McGregor
John R. Meyer
James P. Montgomery
Norman A. Nystrom
Willaim E. Sandvig
Robert L. Showalter
Robert L. Tice
Marianne G. Vethacke
Fern L. Wilson

October 1972

James L. Agee, Chairman
Leroy F. Mumford, President
John Loomer, Vice President
Ruth C. McPhetridge,
  Vice President
Marianne G. Vethacke,
  Vice President

172

Lorrie Gustin, Secretary
Alec S. Lubnik, Treasurer
Witold T. Sikorski,
  Assistant Treasurer
Warren B. Alexander
Duane S. Carr
Cynthia P. Charles
Vernon Cooper
David M. Crowley
Marion W. Dickey
Leland B. Finkbeiner
Robert E. Fletcher
Leon E. Hoffer
William P. McGregor
John R. Meyer
James P. Montgomery
Norman A. Nystrom
Leonard I. Reiser
Dorwin E. Robinson
William E. Sandvig
Robert L. Showalter
Robert L. Tice
Fern L. Wilson

October 1973

James L. Agee, Chairman
Leroy F. Mumford, President
John Loomer, Vice President
Ruth C. McPhetridge,
  Vice President
William E. Sandvig,
  Vice President
Lorrie Gustin, Secretary
Alec S. Lubnik, Treasurer

Witold T. Sikorski,
  Assistant Treasurer
Lee W. Branch
Duane S. Carr
Cynthia P. Charles
Vernon Cooper
Marion W. Dickey
Leland B. Finkbeiner
Robert E. Fletcher
Leon E. Hoffer
Richard G. Horak
William P. McGregor
John R. Meyer
James P. Montgomery
Dorwin E. Robinson
Robert L. Showalter
Robert L. Tice
Fern L. Wilson
  (Deceased, December 1974)

October 1974

James L. Agee, Chairman
Leroy F. Mumford, President
Ruth C. McPhetridge,
  Vice President
William E. Sandvig,
  Vice President
Robert L. Tice, Vice President
Lorrie Gustin, Secretary
Witold T. Sikorski, Treasurer
John Loomer, Assistant Treasurer
Melvin H. Barrett
Edward Bierman
Lee W. Branch
Cynthia P. Charles

173

Vernon Cooper
Marion W. Dickey
Leon E. Hoffer
Richard G. Horak
William P. McGregor
John R. Meyer
James P. Montgomery
Dorwin E. Robinson
Robert L. Showalter

October 1975

James L. Agee, Chairman
Leroy F. Mumford, President
Ruth C. McPhetridge,
  Vice President
William E. Sandvig,
  Vice President
Robert L. Tice, Vice President
Lorrie Gustin, Secretary
Witold T. Sikorski, Treasurer
John Loomer, Assistant Treasurer
Melvin H. Barrett
Edward Bierman
Lee W. Branch
Cynthia P. Charles
Vernon Cooper
Leon E. Hoffer
Richard G. Horak
Alec Lubnik
William P. McGregor
John R. Meyer
James P. Montgomery
Dorwin E. Robinson
Robert L. Sholwater

October 1976

Leroy F. Mumford, Chairman
William E. Sandvig, President
Richard G. Horak, Vice President
John R. Meyer, Vice President
Robert L. Tice, Vice President
Lorrie Gustin, Secretary
John Loomer, Treasurer
James L. Agee
Melvin H. Barrett
Edward Bierman
Lee W. Branch
Cynthia P. Charles
Vernon Cooper
Ruth C. McPhetridge
James P. Montgomery
Dorwin E. Robinson
Robert L. Showalter
Witold T. Sikorski
Juanita G. Swedenburg

October 1977

Leroy F. Mumford, Chairman
William E. Sandvig, President
Richard G. Horak, Vice President
John R. Meyer, Vice President
Robert L. Tice, Vice President
Lorrie Gustin, Secretary
John Loomer, Treasurer
James L. Agee
Edward Bierman
Cynthia P. Charles
Vernon Cooper
John G. Hicks
Dorwin E. Robinson

Robert L. Showalter
Witold T. Sikorski
Juanita G. Swedenburg

October 1978

Leroy F. Mumford, Chairman
William E. Sandvig, President
Cynthia P. Charles, Vice President
Robert L. Tice, Vice President
Lorrie Gustin, Secretary
John Loomer, Treasurer
James L. Agee
Edward Bierman
John G. Hicks
Richard G. Horak
John R. Meyer
Robert L. Showalter
Witold T. Sikorski
Juanita G. Swedenburg

October 1979

Leroy F. Mumford, Chairman
Lorrie Gustin, President
Cynthia P. Charles, Vice President
Robert L. Tice, Vice President
John G. Hicks, Secretary
Richard G. Horak, Treasurer
James L. Agee
Edward Bierman
John R. Meyer
William E. Sandvig
Peggy L. Schmeltz
Robert L. Showalter
Witold T. Sikorski
William F. Strother
Juanita G. Swedenburg

October 1980

Leroy F. Mumford, Chairman
Lorrie Gustin, President
Cynthia P. Charles, Vice President
Robert L. Tice, Vice President
John G. Hicks, Secretary
Richard G. Horak, Treasurer
James L. Agee
Edward Bierman
Chester A. Baker
John M. Paterson
Peggy L. Schmeltz
Robert L. Showalter
Witold T. Sikorski
William F. Strother

October 1981

Leroy F. Mumford, Chairman
Lorrie Gustin, President
William F. Strother, Vice President
Robert L. Tice, Vice President
John G. Hicks, Secretary
Richard G. Horak, Treasurer
James L. Agee
Edward Bierman
Chester A. Baker
Cynthia P. Charles
Ruth C. McPhetridge
John M. Paterson
Peggy L. Schmeltz
Robert L. Showalter
Witold T. Sikorski

175

October 1982

Leroy F. Mumford, Chairman
Lorrie Gustin, President
William F. Strother, Vice President
Robert L. Tice, Vice President
John G. Hicks, Secretary
Richard G. Horak, Treasurer
Edward Bierman
Chester A. Baker
Cynthia P. Charles
Ruth C. McPhetridge
John M. Paterson
Carol J. Pearson
Peggy L. Schmeltz
Robert L. Showalter
Witold T. Sikorski

October 1983

Cynthia P. Charles, Chairman
John M. Paterson, President
William F. Strother, Vice President
Chester A. Baker, Secretary
Edward Bierman, Treasurer
John G. Hicks
Richard G. Horak
Leroy F. Mumford
Carol J. Pearson
Peggy L. Schmeltz
Robert L. Showalter
Robert L. Tice

October 1984

Cynthia P. Charles, Chairman
John M. Paterson, President
William F. Strother, Vice President
Chester A. Baker, Secretary
Edward Bierman, Treasurer
John G. Hicks
Richard G. Horak
Ruth C. McPhetridge
Carol J. Pearson
Peggy L. Schmeltz
Robert L. Showalter
Robert L. Tice
Lennart H. Width

October 1985

Cynthia P. Charles, Chairman
John M. Paterson, President
Chester A. Baker, Vice President
Robert L. Tice, Vice President
Richard G. Horak, Secretary
Edward Bierman, Treasurer
Kenneth H. Erickson
John G. Hicks
Rose C. Kapranos
Ruth C. McPhetridge
Carol J. Pearson
Peggy L. Schmeltz
Robert L. Showalter
William F. Strother
Lennart H. Width

October 1986

Cynthia P. Charles, Chairman
Kenneth H. Erickson, President
Carol J. Pearson, Vice President
Robert L. Tice, Vice President
Richard G. Horak, Secretary
Edward Bierman, Treasurer
Chester A. Baker
John G. Hicks
Rose C. Kapranos
Ruth C. McPhetridge
John M. Paterson
Peggy L. Schmeltz
Robert L. Showalter
William F. Strother
Lennart H. Width

October 1987

Richard G. Horak, Chairman
Robert L. Tice, President
Edward Bierman, Vice President
Kenneth H. Erickson,
  Vice President
Carol J. Pearson, Vice President
John M. Paterson, Secretary
Lennart H. Width, Treasurer
Mary Ann S. Brown
Cynthia P. Charles
John G. Hicks
Rose C. Kapranos
Ruth C. McPhetridge
Peggy L. Schmeltz
William F. Strother
Jerrie Wakeen

October 1988

Richard G. Horak, Chairman
Robert L. Tice, President
Edward Bierman, Vice President
Kenneth H. Erickson,
  Vice President
Carol J. Pearson, Vice President
Rose C. Kapranos, Secretary
Lennart H. Width, Treasurer
Mary Ann S. Brown
Cynthia P. Charles
John G. Hicks
Ruth C. McPhetridge
Peggy L. Schmeltz
William F. Strother
Jerrie Wakeen

October 1989

Richard G. Horak, Chairman
Robert L. Tice, President
John M. Paterson, Vice President
Carol J. Pearson, Vice President
Rose C. Kapranos, Secretary
Edward Bierman, Treasurer
Mary Ann S. Brown
Cynthia P. Charles
Susanne Heimbach
John G. Hicks
Ruth C. McPhetridge
Peggy L. Schmeltz
William F. Strother
Betty A. Taylor
Jerrie Wakeen

October 1990

Robert L. Tice, Chairman
Carol J. Pearson, President
Hans D. Steinke, Vice President
Jerrie Wakeen, Vice President
Lennart H. Width, Vice President
Rose C. Kapranos, Secretary
Edward Bierman, Treasurer
Mary Ann S. Brown
Cynthia P. Charles
Richard G. Horak
Philip J. Keating
Ruth C. McPhetridge
John M. Paterson
Peggy L. Schmeltz
William F. Strother
Betty A. Taylor
Billy M. Williams

October 1991

Robert L. Tice, Chairman
Carol J. Pearson, President
John M. Paterson, Vice President
Jerrie Wakeen, Vice President
Lennart H. Width, Vice President
Rose C. Kapranos, Secretary
Edward Bierman, Treasurer
Mary Ann S. Brown
Cynthia P. Charles
Richard G. Horak
Philip J. Keating
Ruth C. McPhetridge
Hans D. Steinke
Peggy L. Schmeltz
William F. Strother

Betty A. Taylor
Billy M. Williams

October 1992

Robert L. Tice, Chairman
Peggy L. Schmeltz, President
Ruth C. McPhetridge,
  Vice President
Billy M. Williams, Vice President
Lennart H. Width, Secretary
Rose C. Kapranos, Treasurer
Mary Ann S. Brown
Joan Estep
Gordon L. Hakes
Shirley Knudsen
Carol J. Pearson
Robert L. Showalter
William F. Strother
Betty A. Taylor
Jerrie Wakeen-Pittenger

October 1993

Peggy L. Schmeltz, Chairman
Ruth C. McPhetridge, President
Betty A. Taylor, Vice President
Billy M. Williams, Vice President
Lennart H. Width, Secretary
Rose C. Kapranos, Treasurer
William P. Agster
James E. Black
Joan Estep
Gordon L. Hakes
Shirley Knudsen
Carol J. Pearson
Katherine Philipp

178

Elizabeth A. Sinnock
Robert L. Showalter
Robert L. Tice

October 1994

Peggy L. Schmeltz, Chairman
Ruth C. McPhetridge, President
Betty A. Taylor, Vice President
Billy M. Williams, Vice President
Elizabeth A. Sinnock, Secretary
Rose C. Kapranos, Treasurer
William P. Agster
Gary V. Ball
Stephen W. Beer
James E. Black
Gordon L. Hakes
Shirley Knudsen
Carol J. Pearson
Katherine Philipp
Robert L. Showalter
Robert L. Tice
Lennart H. Width
Lorna Daniels, Associate
Edward Bierman, Associate
Emma Dimpfel, Associate
Evonne A. Hurst, Associate
Larry Reno, Associate
Ingeborg T. Steinke, Associate
Anne L. Uno, Associate

October 1995

Peggy L. Schmeltz, Chairman
Ruth C. McPhetridge, President
Rose C. Kapranos, Vice President
Betty A. Taylor, Vice President

James E. Black, Secretary
Elizabeth A. Sinnock, Treasurer
William P. Agster
Gary V. Ball
Stephen W. Beer
Robert V. Blailock
Emma Dimpfel
Gordon L. Hakes
Evonne A. Hurst
Katherine Philipp
Lennart H. Width
Billy M. Williams
Kenneth H. Erickson, Associate
Shirley Knudsen, Associate
JoAnn Linck, Associate
Ingeborg T. Steinke, Associate
Anne L. Uno, Associate

October 1996

Ruth C. McPhetridge, Chairman
Rose C. Kapranos, President
Stephen W. Beer, Vice President
Evonne A. Hurst, Vice President
Elizabeth A. Sinnock, Secretary
Shirley Knudsen, Treasurer
William P. Agster
Gary V. Ball
Robert V. Blailock
Christine G. Curtis
Emma Dimpfel
Gordon L. Hakes
JoAnn Linck
Mary L. Reynolds
William A. Sacre
Betty A. Taylor

179

Saundra Wall Williams
Robert S. Kovach, Associate
Carol J. Pearson, Associate
Ingeborg T. Steinke, Associate
Anne A. Uno, Associate

October 1997

Ruth C. McPhetridge, Chairman
Shirley Knudsen, President
Evonne A. Hurst, Vice President
William A. Sacre, Vice President
Elizabeth A. Sinnock, Secretary
Robert V. Blailock, Treasurer
William P. Agster
Gary V. Ball
Christine G. Curtis
Emma Dimpfel
Gordon L. Hakes
Donna Jones
JoAnn Linck
Carol J. Pearson
Mary L. Reynolds
Betty A. Taylor
Billy M. Williams
Saundra Wall Williams
Stephen W. Beer, Associate
Rose C. Kapranos, Associate
Robert S. Kovach, Associate
Larry Reno, Associate
Ingeborg T. Steinke, Associate
Anne A. Uno, Associate

October 1998

Ruth C. McPhetridge, Chairman
Shirley Knudsen, President
Evonne A. Hurst, Vice President
William A. Sacre, Vice President
Elizabeth A. Sinnock, Secretary
Robert B. Blailock, Treasurer
William P. Agster
Gary V. Ball
Christine G. Curtis
Emma Dimpfel
Gordon L. Hakes
Donna Jones
JoAnn Linck
Carol J. Pearson
Mary L. Reynolds
Betty A. Taylor
Billy M. Williams
Saundra Wall Williams
Stephen W. Beer, Associate
Jennifer Evans, Associate
Rose C. Kapranos, Associate
Robert S. Kovach, Associate
Larry Reno, Associate
Ingeborg, T. Steinke, Associate
Anne A. Uno, Associate

October 1999

Shirley Knudsen, Chairman
William A. Sacre, President
Christine G. Curtis, Vice President
Gordon L. Hakes, Vice President
JoAnn Linck, Secretary
Robert V. Blailock, Treasurer
William P. Agster
Gary V. Ball
Stephen W. Beer
Emma Dimpfel
Evonne A. Hurst
Donna Jones
Carol J. Pearson
Dorothy Rauschelbach
Mary L. Reynolds
Quentin R. Sampson
Elizabeth A. Sinnock
Billy M. Williams
Saundra Wall Williams
Pat Wood
Mary Lyn Goerke, Associate
Kenneth Kern, Associate
Hugh McManus, Associate
Monica Noel, Assocciate
Jennifer Evans, Assistant
Robert S. Kovach. Assistant
Larry Reno, Assistant
Ingeborg T. Steinke, Assistant
Anne A. Uno, Assistant

September 2000

Shirley Knudsen, Chairman
Christine G. Curtis, President
Gary V. Ball, Vice President
Elizabeth A. Sinnock,
   Vice President
JoAnn Linck, Secretary
Robert V. Blailock, Treasurer
William P. Agster
Stephen W. Beer
Emma Dimpfel
Mary Lyn Goerke
Evonne A. Hurst
Donna Jones
Hugh McManus
Dorothy Rauschelbach
Larry Reno
Quentin R. Sampson
Billy M. Williams
Saundra Wall Williams
Pat Wood
Linda Blay, Associate
Carol Haverty, Associate
Patrick Connell, Associate
Monica Noel, Associate
Jennifer Evans, Assistant
Robert S. Kovach, Assistant
Ingeborg T. Steinke, Assistant
Anne A. Uno, Assistant

181

As computers have advanced in capability, NAIC members have learned to use them to analyze individual corporations via a computerized program of NAIC's Stock Selection Guide and Report. Computers provide access to tremendous amounts of information about individual corporations and their respective industries to help members make more informed decisions. In 1985 the Trustees approved a new division to concentrate the Association's development in the computer area.

Computer Group

First Computer Group Board
1988-89

John M. Paterson, Chairman
Philip J. Keating,
  First Vice President
Robert Kalischer,
  Second Vice President
Bruce H. Wagner,
  Secretary-Treasurer
Donald E. Danko
Richard Kenfield
John Snider

1989-90

John M. Paterson, Chairman
Philip J. Keating,
  First Vice President
Robert Kalischer,
  Second Vice President
Bruce H. Wagner,
  Secretary-Treasurer
Donald E. Danko
Robert DeCrick
Richard A. Dwyer
Richard Kenfield

1990-91

John M. Paterson, Chairman
Philip J. Keating, President
Bruce H. Wagner,
  Secretary-Treasurer
Donald E. Danko
Robert DeCrick
Richard A. Dwyer
Richard Kenfield
Ellis Traub

1991-92

Philip J. Keating, Chairman
Donald E. Danko, President
Bruce H. Wagner,
  Secretary-Treasurer
Robert DeCrick
Richard Kenfield
Donald Scidmore
Hans D. Steinke
Betty A. Taylor

182

Ellis Traub
Christopher T. Collins, Associate
Jerome C. Cooper, Associate
Elizabeth Hart, Associate
Jeanne Squires, Associate
Ingeborg T. Steinke, Associate

1992-93

Philip J. Keating, Chairman
Donald E. Danko, President
Ellis Traub, Secretary
Christopher T. Collins, Treasurer
Jerome C. Cooper
Richard Kenfield
Donald Scidmore
Hans D. Steinke
Bruce H. Wagner
Robert Adams, Associate
Herbert K. Barnett, Associate
Robert DeCrick, Associate
Kenneth C. Halwas, Associate
Elizabeth Hart, Associate
Jeanne Squires, Associate
Michael Stigall, Associate

1993-94

Philip J. Keating, Chairman
Richard Kenfield, President
Jerome C. Cooper, Vice President
Hans D. Steinke, Vice President
Herbert K. Barnett, Secretary
Christopher T. Collins, Treasurer
Donald E. Danko
Elizabeth Hunt
Ellis Traub

Bruce H. Wagner
Robert Adams, Associate
Edgar D. Berners, Associate
Corry Dal Maso, Associate
Kenneth C. Halwas, Associate
Michael Stigall, Associate
William C. Thomas, Associate
Werner H. Wahl, Associate

1994-95

Philip J. Keating, Chairman
Herbert K. Barnett, President
Jerome C. Cooper, Vice President
Hans D. Steinke, Vice President
William C. Thomas, Secretary
Christopher T. Collins, Treasurer
Edgar D. Berners
Donald E. Danko
Bruce H. Wagner
Robert Adams, Associate
Richard D. Becker, Associate
Joseph N. Craig, Associate
Kenneth C. Halwas, Associate
Gizella Keating, Associate
Kenneth J. Morris, Associate
G. Kenneth Wood, Associate

1995-96

Philip J. Keating, Chairman
Herbert K. Barnett, President
Hans D. Steinke, Vice President
William C. Thomas, Secretary
Werner H. Wahl, Treasurer
Richard D. Becker
Christopher T. Collins

Jerome C. Cooper
Joseph H. Craig
Kenneth J. Morris
G. Kenneth Wood
Robert Adams, Associate
Mary Ann Davis, Associate
Douglas Gerlach, Associate
Kenneth A. Halwas, Associate
Gizella Keating, Associate
Phyllis G. Pawlovsky, Associate
Joan L. Pringle, Associate

1996-97

Herbert K. Barnett, Chairman
William C. Thomas, President
Joseph H. Craig, Vice President
Kenneth J. Morris, Secretary
Werner H. Wahl, Treasurer
Richard D. Becker
Christopher T. Collins
Jerome C. Cooper
Mary Ann Davis
Douglas Gerlach
Philip J. Keating
Hans D. Steinke
G. Kenneth Wood
Nancy Crays, Associate
Kenneth A. Halwas, Associate
Steve Martin, Associate
Phyllis G. Pawlovsky, Associate
Linda K. Penfold, Associate
Robert Schaelchlin, Associate
Leslie A. Wilkinson, Associate
Bart Womack, Associate

1997-98

Herbert K. Barnett, Chairman
William C. Thomas, President
Joseph N. Craig, Vice President
Kenneth J. Morris, Secretary
Werner H. Wahl, Treasurer
Richard D. Becker
Christopher T. Collins
Mary Ann Davis
Douglas Gerlach
Philip J. Keating
Hans D. Steinke
G. Kenneth Wood
Nancy Crays, Associate
Kenneth A. Halwas, Associate
Steve Martin, Associate
Phyllis G. Pawlovsky, Associate
Linda K. Penfold, Associate
Robert Schaelchlin, Associate
Leslie A. Wilkinson, Associate
Bart Womack, Associate

1998-99

Herbert K. Barnett, Chairman
Joseph N. Craig, President
Kenneth J. Morris, Secretary
Werner H. Wahl, Treasurer
Richard D. Becker
Christopher T. Collins
Mary Ann Davis
Douglas Gerlach
Philip J. Keating
Steve Martin
Robert Schaelchlin
Hans D. Steinke

William C. Thomas
Leslie A. Wilkinson
G. Kenneth Wood
Mac Almond, Associate
Michael C. Bacsa, Associate
Nancy Crays, Associate
Kenneth A. Halwas, Associate
Pat McVey-Ritsick, Associate
Phyllis G. Pawlovsky, Associate
Linda K. Penfold, Associate
Bart Womack, Associate

1999-2000

Herbert K. Barnett, Chairman
Joseph N. Craig, President
Kenneth J. Morris, Secretary
Werner H. Wahl, Treasurer
Michael C. Bacsa
Christopher T. Collins
Nancy Crays
Mary Ann Davis
Douglas Gerlach
Philip J. Keating
Steve Martin
Pat McVey-Ritsick
Phyllis G. Pawlovsky
Robert Schaelchlin
Hans D. Steinke
William C. Thomas
Leslie A. Wilkinson
G. Kenneth Woods
Robert Adams, Associate
Sandra Barlow, Associate
Jerry Dressel, Associate
Kenneth A. Halwas, Associate

Cyrell E. Lynch, Associate
Linda K. Penfold, Associate
Bart Womack, Associate
Pam Wright, Associate

2000-01

Werner H. Wahl, Chairman
Joseph N. Craig, President
Douglas Gerlach, Secretary
Robert Schaelchlin, Treasurer
Robert Adams
Michael C. Bacsa
Sandra Barlow
Herbert K. Barnett
Christopher T. Collins
Nancy Crays
Mary Ann Davis
Cyrell E. Lynch
Steve Martin
Pat McVey-Ritsick
Kenneth J. Morris
Phyllis G. Pawlovsky
  (Resigned, August 2000)
Hans D. Steinke
William C. Thomas
G. Kenneth Wood
Pam Wright
Kathleen Boettcher, Associate
Nance deGraff, Associate
Diane Graese, Associate
Kenneth A. Halwas, Associate
Seymour Zeenkov, Associate

185

Appendix B

The Investment Education Institute was a dream of George A. Nicholson, Jr. It was conceived as another way to involve more parts of society in the task of bringing investment education to the masses.

George believed that business, the government and the educational establishment all benefit from a population with a strong measure of investment education. If a large portion of the population understands the value and importance of the free market economy in building the most efficient economic system, and providing the highest standard of living for every citizen, these major parts of society would benefit from a less fettered free market system and broader potential support.

NAIC's Board of Trustees agreed with George's idea and started NAIC on a movement to raise funds to support the starting of NAIC's Investment Education Institute. Frederick Brownell, a prominent public relations executive in Detroit and an NAIC supporter, volunteered to write the brochure for the fund-raising program. His work was very effective and produced a little over $20,000 from the first mailing, but it was difficult to keep interest active and the fund raising was discontinued after three years and the receipt of $50,000.

That wasn't a barn-burning success, but George and the rest of us had come up with some ideas we started to put into effect. George wanted to set up an organization of business, government and educational leaders who would work to develop investment education programs in their respective areas. We decided to seek the support of the Wayne State University Business School to arrange conferences with leaders in the three groups to see if effective groups could be set up in the three areas to develop continuing investment education programs.

Several NAIC trustees were almuni of Wayne State University and visited Dr. Bruce C. DeSpelder, a Business School Professor at Wayne and a fraternity brother to explain our objective and see if we

186

could obtain his and the university's help in organizing and staging the three conferences. In a short time, Bruce advised us he would be pleased to help and that the Dean had approved the University's participation. The funds raised were transferred to the University under the direction of Dr. DeSpelder.

We decided to organize business people first. There was a new profession developing in the corporate world, a corporation's executive in charge of share owner relations. At that time there were probably less than ten corporations that had a department assigned to that task. In more cases, that job was just developing and was a part-time assignment of the treasurer or secretary. We surmised that this person would likely be the individual in the corporation with the greatest interest in investment education. The first conference was set for July 27, 1962 at Wayne's new McGregor Conference Center. Thirty-nine attended the meeting and a high level of interest resulted in plans for a follow-up meeting. By the fourth conference, held June 17-19, 1968, almost two hundred attended. NAIC had frequently advised the conference attendees that the one purpose of the meetings was to persuade the stockholder relation's executives to form their own professional organization. A group of them had started meeting together and called themselves the Investor Relations Institute and were sponsors of the fourth conference with NAIC and Wayne State University.

As we started planning a fifth conference, the Investor Relations Institute informed us they were forming a national professional organization. They requested that we call off our scheduled fifth conference. Our mission was accomplished and we were happy to see the new group, now known as the National Investor Relations Institute, take over the future. It has been very successful and has worked for a steady increase in the amount of investment information available to the individual investor.

We were not as successful with our efforts to form a new educational and government group. With Wayne State University assisting, two conferences were held for educators and one for government officials. We were unable to develop interest in creating new organizations in these areas to promote mass investment education, but we did meet a number of individuals who gave valuable suggestions to NAIC.

Dr. DeSpelder, with the help of friends at Wayne State, contributed several items to the growth of NAIC. He conducted research to verify that investment clubs were an effective classroom for investment education. Upon confirming that fact, NAIC concluded its education program would be much more effective if the teaching members of NAIC chapters could be more thoroughly trained. This led to the start of the annual teacher-training program now offered to directors and workers of every chapter. DeSpelder also pre-tested in his classes the effectiveness of NAIC's Stock Comparison form and the Ten Question part of NAIC's Stock Selection Guide and Report.

NAIC recognized that the cause of mass investment education could be advanced if the IEI gave an award to individuals who had made significant monthly contributions. This award is highly prized and is frequently listed in the biographical statements of recipients. The award is called: NAIC's Investment Education Institute's Distinguished Service Award in Investment Education. The award is made for service in different areas of investment education. The awards were first present 1963. Following is the list of awardees through the year 2001.

Investment Education Institute Winners – Through 2001

FINANCIAL ANALYSTS

Ralph Acampora 1997
David Babson 1965
Arnold Bernhard 1970
Robert Bilkie 2000
George Bissell 1970
Frank Capiello 1981
C. Sidney Cottle 1971
Robert Driscoll 1973
Mary Farrell 1982

James Fraser 1977
Lucien Hooper 1970
Arvid Jouppi 1979
Walter Kirchberger 1990
A. Moyer Kulp 1964
Gerald Loeb 1972
Peter Lynch 1993
George Nicholson 1964
William Norby 1967
Thomas O'Hara 1969

Patricia Peacock 1983	**INVESTMENT CLUBS**
H. Bradlee Perry 1985	James Agee 1981
Charles Ricker 1979	William Agster. 1996
Stephen Sanborn 1999	Warren Alexander 1979
Elliott Schlang 1992	The Beardstown Ladies. . 1995
Robert Taylor. 1981	Robert Burger 1975
John Templeton 1988	Cynthia Charles 1977
David Wendell. 1980	Christine Curtis 2000
John Westergaard. 1978	Grafton Daniels 1998
	Donald Danko 1988
	Marion Dickey. 1973
PUBLICATIONS	Emma Dimpfel 1994
Charles Allmon 1971	Kenneth Erickson 1977
Mark Appleman. 1979	Lee Finkbeiner. 1976
Alexandra Armstrong . . 1993	Robert Fletcher 1972
Robert Blieberg 1986	Henry Ford 1987
John Bryan 1965	Deborah Fraser 1990
John Cunniff 1977	Wagar Glas 1970
Nancy Dunnan. 1991	Lorrie Gustin 1973
John Hazard. 1968	Robert Hague 1994
Mark Hulbert. 1992	Jerome Henry 1979
Roger Ibbotson 1986	Frances Hughes 1992
Paula Kent. 1969	Kenneth Janke 1972
Knight Kipplinger 1992	Sally Janke 1997
Andrew Leckey 1998	Rose Kapranos. 1994
Ben Larson 1969	Shirley Knudsen 1997
J. A. Livingston 1970	Helen McLane. 1968
William Mahoney 1991	Ruth McPhetridge 1999
H. Russell Morrison. . . . 1968	Harry Methner. 1984
Vermont Royster 1966	Lothar Methner 1992
Louis Rukeyser 1983	John Meyer 1970
Merryle Rukeyser 1973	Paul Miller. 1970
William Rukeyser 1981	Leroy Mumford. 1969
Aerlo Sederberg. 1967	Jean Palacz 1971
Sam Shulsky 1966	John Paterson. 1991
Walter Smith 1972	Don & Carol Pearson . . 1993
Rawleigh Warner 1970	

Robert Pryor 1975
LaVonne &
Robert Raney 1992
Leonard Reiser 1985
Lewis Rockwell 1973
Roger Ruch 1991
Fred Russell 1963
William Sandvig 1978
Vernon Schiller 1977
William &
Peggy Schmeltz 1982
Ralph Seger 1967
Robert Showalter 1978
Leon Straub 1992
Betty & Robert Taylor . . 1993
Medora Taylor 1985
Robert Tice 1983
Lennart Width 1988
Fern Wilson 1967

STOCK MARKET
William Batten 1982
James Day 1964
Edwin Ethrington 1966
Keith Funston 1963
Paula Gavin 1995
Richard Grasso 1998
Paul Kolton 1990
Arthur Levitt, Jr. 1979
Rudd Lawrence 1968
Gordon Macklin 1983
James Needham 1975
John Phelan 1987
Michael Tobin 1972

GOVERNMENT
Arthur Burns 1976
Alden Clausen 1983
Gerald R. Ford 1993
Howard Jarvis 1978
Lyndon B. Johnson 1965
John F. Kennedy 1963
Otto Kerner 1967
Paul McCracken 1969
Wilbur Mills 1976
Richard M. Nixon 1972
Robert Rubin 1999
Martha Seger 1987
John S. R. Shad 1973
Nancy Smith 2000
David Stockman 1981

INDUSTRY
John Amos 1986
Warren Buffett 1989
Walker Cisler 1965
Virginia Dwyer 1981
Henry Ford II. 1968
B. S. Gilmer 1969
J. Peter Grace 1983
Raymond Hagel 1990
Fred Hartley 1969
Ernest Henderson 1963
J. M. (Mac) Hill 1982
Ed Johnson 1973
Lawrence Jones 1987
James Karman 1990
Thomas McCabe 1964
Thomas Murphy 1977
Alan E. Murray 1988
Guy Pepiatt 1966

Michael Quinlan 1997
Thomas Russell 1984
Charles Thronton 1967
James Walter 1977
C. V. Wood 1970
Walter Wriston 1993
D. Craig Yessee 1981

EDUCATORS/
ECONOMISTS

David Bunting 1967
Bruce DeSpelder 1971
Constantinos Doxiadis . . 1966
Milton Friedman 1968
Benjamin Graham 1963
Merrill Griswold 1963
Rolland Hallquist 1975
Arthur Laffer 1981
Alice McKee 1985
Joan Morrissey 1993
John Pfahl 1965
Wiley Pickett 1982
Paul Samuelson 1973
Harry Sauvain 1964
Joseph Schumpeter 1970

INVESTOR RELATIONS

R. Lee Anderson 1983
J. F. Bradley 1967
Gudrun Carr 1999
William Chatlos 1968
Howard Christensen . . . 1984
Geoffrey Fallon 1988
John Gearhart 1967
William Hartl 1983
Mary Healy 1990

Richard Holthaua 1989
Kenneth Janke, Jr. 2000
Lois Kennedy 1985
Kenneth Lightcap 1989
Eugene Miller 1973
Winthrop Neilson 1986
William Phillips 1972
Charlotte Reeves 1975
Arthur Roalman 1983
O. Glenn Saxon 1964
Katharine Tarbox 1982
Louis Thompson, Jr. . . . 1987
Waid Vanderpoel 1976
Terry Wilson 1981

INTERNATIONAL

John Bart 1996
Kurt Barte 1976
Sir Edward Boyle 1968
E. A. Brouwer 1963
Mdme. D'Estaing 1983
M. R. Dhawan 1963
J. J. DeJong 1969
Joseph Dodge 1970
Ludwig Erhard 1964
Haken Girgils 1979
Waziri Ibrahim 1963
Toshio Inoue 1963
Hans Kloss 1990
William Lowe 1983
John Maes 1973
Birgit Malmestam-Skytt . . 1986
David Moate 1963
Rene Monory 1980
Bernard &
Roslyn Pierre 1972

191

C. J. Schimmelpennick . . 1963
Ruppert Siemon. 1973
A. D. H. Smith 1983
Alfred Snutsel 1973
Jan Tinbergen 1963
Claude Vallon 1994
J. J. L. van Berckel 1978
J. W. C. van Langen. . . . 1963
Christian Will 1972
Michel &
Monique Willemaers . . . 1971

COMPUTER GROUP
Herbert Barnett 1997
Edward Chiampi 1986
Joe Craig 1996
Douglas Gerlach 1996
Philip Keating 1992
Cy Lynch. 2000

CORPORATIONS
AFLAC Incorporated. . . 1996

Currently the activities of the IEI are directed at building the Youth Investment Education program of NAIC and a program to give a large number of teachers each year special training in the teaching of tested long-term investment principles. Grant money is being sought to enlarge this program.

Appendix C

Much of NAIC's success has come from the large number of volunteers who have served the organization. Each one has made a solid contribution to building the organization we have today.

For the first six years of NAIC's existence, everyone was a volunteer. While secretaries were employed about a year into NAIC's life, it was not until 1958 that a more extensive staff was hired. While records of the early Chapters are not complete, it is easy to see that to date more than six thousand individuals have worked in various volunteer capacities to operate NAIC. Today, there are just under three thousand serving in all parts of the organization. Their work has contributed to the investment knowledge of over three million people.

We hesitate to name individuals for special accomplishment because we are very likely to miss a number that were of great help, but believe it is important to record as many as we can remember.

NAIC's first volunteer was Lewis A. Rockwell. Lew volunteered to write the Trust Agreement that marked the founding of NAIC. The outline was provided by George A. Nicholson, Jr. but Lew gave it body. In time Rockwell became NAIC's attorney and helped it attain tax-exempt staus.

Wagar Glass was a member of one of the founding clubs, The One Hundred Ten Club of Ann Arbor, Michigan. Wagar was elected the first Chairman of NAIC's National Board and served until December 1969. He provided a great deal of strength and stability in the organization through those formative years.

Robert L. Pryor, the first Secretary of the Board of Trustees through the six years leading up to NAIC's paid staff oversaw the growing volume of correspondence to be handled. This was a very large task.

Robert A. Burger was the Trust's first Treasurer. In addition, Bob did the first re-write of NAIC's Manual of Club Treasurers and put it in plain English to the great relief of club treasurers.

Paul R. Miller, an executive speech writer at General Motors, was a member of NAIC's Board of Directors in 1952 and volunteered to write NAIC's promotional folder, titled *An Educational and Investment Opportunity for You.* The folder was revised and reprinted as NAIC's major sales piece until 1989.

Ralph L. Seger, Jr. served as a Director of the National Board and was elected a Trustee. Ralph had a special interest in NAIC's stock study procedures and took on the "Repair Shop" column of *Better Investing* when George Nicholson ceased to produce it. He originated the Pert Portfolio Evaluation Review Technique.

Leland B. Finkbeiner was elected a Director of the Michigan Division of NAIC in 1953, later became a National Director and eventually President in 1958. He served until November 1974. His knowledge and experience were of great help to the Board. His organizational ability added greatly to the quality of the National Congress.

Helen J. McLane, an organizer of the Chicago Chapter, was co-author of the first book on Investment Clubs, served as a Director of the National Board, a Trustee and on NAIC's Board of Advisors. She rewrote NAIC's Investors Manual and authored NAIC's first Mutual Fund Manual and Mutual Fund Study Forms.

James L. Agee served in every office in the Detroit Chapter and established a practice of following all new attendees at the Chapter to determine their possible interest in serving in Chapter leadership positions. He initiated the first all-day Saturday program for the Chapter as a forerunner of the Chapter Fair program. Jim also served on the National Boards as Director and President.

Leroy F. Mumford was a co-founder of the Northeast Ohio Chapter and led it to become an example to many new Chapters. He became a National Director and Chairman of the Board where he exhibited the same organizational skills. He formed his own meeting planning company and managed the National Congress for many years. The same organization undertook to organize new Chapters for NAIC and produced considerable growth in new Chapters. Lee became a Trustee.

Lorrie Gustin was a force for the building of the Milwaukee Chapter. As a National Director she gave exceptional leadership to the development of the exhibit area of the National Congress.

She also gave great leadership to the development of the social side of the Congress. Lorrie has also served on the Board of Trustees.

Paul J. Breznen was also a co-founder of the Northeast Ohio Chapter and a leader in developing its programs that made it an example for other Chapters.

James R.S. Millar was a member of the National Board and the second editor of *Better Investing*.

Kenneth Thompson, as financial editor of the *Detroit Free Press*, wrote the article that was very significant in the formation of NAIC and he served as the fourth editor of *Better Investing*.

Ruth C. McPhetridge, was a member of the Cleveland-Akron Chapter and as she traveled with her husband, contributed to Chapters on the East and West Coasts. As a National Board member and Chairman, she greatly assisted in the development of the training program for Chapter members staged by the National Board.

William E. Sandvig was a member of the Twin Cities Chapter. He became a National Board member and later its Chairman. He was a co-originator and developer of the Investors Fair program that has been the most effective program staged by Chapters and their best funding source.

Robert E. Tice started as a member of the Northeast Ohio Chapter and moved quickly to a leadership position on the National Board. He had an exceptional talent for organization and detail and helped make NAIC's annual Congress an exceptionally smooth operation. The same talent helped him become a leader in the formation of new Chapters.

Kenneth H. Erickson served the Minneapolis-St. Paul Chapter and the National Board. He was a co-originator of the Investors Fair program for Chapters making a major contribution to the development of NAIC's Chapters.

Lennart H. Width developed a survey of his Seattle Chapter that attracted the attention of the press and led to exceptional publicity for the Chapter. Len used that publicity to help new clubs in the Chapter. This was the most successful new club-building program ever developed by a Chapter and resulted in an unusually high number of clubs in his area.

Peggy L. Schmeltz was very effective in building the Northwest Ohio Chapter with her unique ability to place the right person in the right place. Upon her husband's retirement, the Schmetlzes were engaged in a program of teaching to the armed forces that took them, not only all over the country, but around the world. They brought NAIC Stock Study Procedures to every class. Peggy has continued her speaking mission and has been one of the most effective individuals in spreading the NAIC story.

John Paterson was an able organization builder. He was very effective in the Seattle Chapter. One of the first to recognize the ability of computers to make investing easier, Paterson developed a program to handle club accounting. He took the lead in directing the efforts of the National Board to develop computer-backed activities and, when appointed to set up a Computer Group, established that Group on a sound organizational basis.

William Agster noticed that the first ten securities in NAIC's annual Top One Hundred Stocks owned by NAIC members had a very good record. He suggested NAIC make an index of the Top One Hundred as representative of the holdings of NAIC members. That index has become the key indicator of the earning performance of NAIC members.

Betty A. Taylor became a leader and helped raise the level of teaching in our Chapters' trainer level, as NAIC moved into a greatly enlarged program of training Chapter Directors as teachers.

Betty A. Sinnock was a founder of the Beardstown Ladies Investment Club and a leader of the club through the years as it became the best known women's investment club in the world. In all their public appearances she and the other members of the club gave credit to NAIC for their success. The publicity they directed at NAIC in the 1990s pushed NAIC to record membership levels and showed literally millions of individuals that they could be successful investors starting with very little money or experience.

William A. Sacre, having seen the success of Lennart Width in building his Chapter's membership, used frequent Own Your Share of America presentations to attract individuals and lead hundreds of individuals to a knowledge of profitable stock selection procedures.

Appendixes B & C have given you the names of some of the individuals who have helped NAIC become the premier investment education organization that it is today. New volunteers are joining the ranks every hour to carry forward the NAIC goal of helping everyone become a successful and lifetime investor.

The publication of this book coordinated by
The Larson Communications Group

Cover and illustrations by Margot Johnston

Production by John Harris/HelioGraphics